PAUL & CARO
WILLCO

C000255061

NORMANDY
AND
THE SEINE

NORMANDY
AND
THE SEINE

Translated by Helen McPhail
Translation co-ordinator Ros Schwartz

Robertson McCarta

The publishers thank the following people for their help with this book: Isabelle Daguin, Philippe Lambert, Vicky Hayward, Gianna Rossi, Sally MacEachern, Helen Beltran, Tessa Hatts

First published in 1989 by

Robertson McCarta Limited
122 King's Cross Road,
London WC1X 9DS

in association with

Fédération Française de Randonnée Pédestre
8 Avenue Marceau
75008 Paris

© Robertson McCarta Limited
© Fédération Française de Randonnée Pédestre
© Maps, Institut Geographique National (French Official Survey)
    and Robertson McCarta Limited.

Managing Editor Jackie Jones
Designed by Prue Bucknall
Production by Grahame Griffiths
Typeset by Columns of Reading
Planning Map by Robertson Merlin

Printed and bound in Hong Kong

This book is sold subject to the condition that it shall not, by way of trade of otherwise, be lent, resold, hired out, or otherwise circulated without the publisher's prior consent in any form of binding or cover other than that in which it is published and without a similar condition including this condition being imposed on the subsequent purchaser.

British Library Cataloguing in Publication Data

Normandy and the Seine — (Footpaths of Europe)
    1. France. Normandy. Visitors' guides
    I. McPhail, Helen   II. Series
    796.5'1'09442

ISBN 1—85365—155—9

Every care has been taken to ensure that all the information in this book is accurate. The publishers cannot accept any responsibility for any errors that may appear or their consequences.

CONTENTS

Walk 1   18

Rouen ▶ *GR25d* ▶ Bois-Isambert ▶ *GR25* ▶ Le Bout-de-la-Côte ▶
GR25 ▶ Bourg-Joly ▶ *GR2* ▶ **Duclair**

Walk 2   24

Duclair ▶ *GR23a* ▶ Bac-de-Jumièges ▶ *GR23* ▶ **Tancarville**

Walk 3   32

Triel ▶ *GR2* ▶ Sotteville-sous-le-Val ▶ *GR2* ▶ La Bouille ▶ *GR2* ▶
Duclair ▶ *GR2* ▶ *Caudebec-en-Caux* ▶ *GR2* ▶ Tancarville ▶ *GR2*
▶ Montivilliers ▶ *GR2* ▶ **Le Havre**

Walk 4   96

Rouen ▶ *GR25a & 25* ▶ **Sotteville-sous-le-Val**

Walk 5   100

Caudebec-en-Caux ▶ *GR211* ▶ **Veulettes-sur-Mer**

Walk 6   110

Sainte-Marguerite ▶ *GR212* ▶ **Le Bout-de-la-Côte**

Walk 7   118

Le Havre ▶ *GR2* ▶ Montivilliers ▶ *GR21* ▶ Veulettes-sur-Mer ▶ *GR21*
▶ Sainte-Marguerite ▶ *GR21* ▶ **Dieppe**

A note from the publisher

The books in this French Walking Guide series are published in association and with the help of the Fédération Française de la Randonnée Pédestre (French ramblers' association) — generally known as the FFRP.

The FFRP is a federal organisation and is made up of regional, local and many other associations and bodies that form its constituent parts. Individual membership is through these various local organisations. The FFRP therefore acts as an umbrella organisation overseeing the waymarking of footpaths, training and the publishing of the Topoguides, detailed guides to the Grande Randonnée footpaths.

There are at present about 170 Topoguides in print, compiled and written by local members of the FFRP, who are responsible for waymarking the walks — so they are well researched and accurate.

We have translated the main itinerary descriptions, amalgamating and adapting several Topoguides to create new regional guides. We have retained the basic Topoguide structure, indicating length and times of walks, and the Institut Géographique National (official French survey) maps overlaid with the routes.

The information contained in this guide is the latest available at the time of going to print. However, as publishers we are aware that this kind of information is continually changing and we are anxious to enhance and improve the guides as much as possible. We encourage you to send us suggestions, criticisms and those little bits of information you may wish to share with your fellow walkers. Our address is: Robertson-McCarta, 122 King's Cross Road, London WC1X 9DS.

We shall be happy to offer a free copy of any one of these books to any reader whose suggestions are subsequently incorporated into a new edition.

It is possible to create a variety of routes by referring to the walks above and to the planning map (inside the front cover). Transport and accommodation are listed in the alphabetical index at the back of the book.

KEY

Gournay

This example shows that it is 7km from Gournay to Arbois, and that you can expect it to take 2 hours, 10 minutes.

7Km
2:10

ARBOIS
🏠 ⛺ ✕ 🏪 🚌
14th century church

Arbois has a variety of facilities, including hotels and buses. Hotel addresses and bus/train connections may be listed in the index at the back of the book.

a grey arrow indicates an alternative route that leaves and returns to the main route.

Detour

indicates a short detour off the route to a town with facilities or to an interesting sight.

Symbols:

🏠 hotel;
🏠 youth hostel, hut or refuge;
⛺ camping;
✕ restaurant;
🍸 cafe;

🏪 shops;
🚃 railway station;
🚌 buses;
⛴ ferry;
🅸 tourist information.

THE FOOTPATHS OF FRANCE

by Robin Neillands

Why should you go walking in France? Well, walking is fun and as for France, Danton summed up the attractions of that country with one telling phrase: 'Every man has two countries,' he said, 'his own . . . and France.' That is certainly true in my case and I therefore consider it both a pleasure and an honour to write this general introduction to these footpath guides to France. A pleasure because walking in or through France is my favourite pastime, an honour because these excellent English language guides follow in the course set by those Topo-guides published in French by the Fédération Française pour la Randonnée Pédestre, which set a benchmark for quality that all footpath guides might follow. Besides, I believe that good things should be shared and walking in France is one of the most pleasant activities I know.

I have been walking in France for over thirty years. I began by rambling — or rather ambling — through the foothills of the Pyrenees, crossing over into Spain past the old Hospice de France, coming back over the Somport Pass in a howling blizzard, which may account for the fact that I totally missed two sets of frontier guards on both occasions. Since then I have walked in many parts of France and even from one end of it to the other, from the Channel to the Camargue, and I hope to go on walking there for many years to come.

The attractions of France are legion, but there is no finer way to see and enjoy them than on foot. France has two coasts, at least three mountain ranges — the Alps, Pyrenees and the Massif Central — an agreeable climate, a great sense of space, good food, fine wines and, believe it or not, a friendly and hospitable people. If you don't believe me, go there on foot and see for yourself. Walking in France will appeal to every kind of walker, from the day rambler to the backpacker, because above all, and in the nicest possible way, the walking in France is well organized, but those Francophiles who already know France well, will find it even more pleasureable if they explore their favourite country on foot.

The GR system

The Grande Randonnée (GR) footpath network now consists of more than 40,000 kilometres (25,000 miles) of long-distance footpath, stretching into every part of France, forming a great sweep around Paris, probing deeply into the Alps, the Pyrenees, and the volcanic cones of the Massif Central. This network, the finest system of footpaths in Europe, is the creation of that marvellously named organization, *la Fédération Française de Randonnée Pédestre, Comité National des Sentiers de Grande Randonnée*, which I shall abbreviate to FFRP-CNSGR. Founded in 1948, and declaring that, *'un jour de marche, huit jours de santé,'* the FFRP-CNSGR has flourished for four decades and put up the now familiar red-and-white waymarks in every corner of the country. Some of these footpaths are classic walks, like the famous GR65, *Le Chemin de St Jacques*, the ancient Pilgrim Road to Compostela, the TMB, the *Tour du Mont Blanc*, which circles the mountain through France, Switzerland and Italy, or the 600-mile long GR3, the *Sentier de la Loire*, which runs from the Ardèche to the Atlantic, to give three examples from the hundred or so GR trails available. In addition there is an abundance of GR du Pays or regional footpaths, like the *Sentier de la Haute Auvergne*, and the *Sentier Tour des Monts d'Aubrac*. A 'Tour' incidentally, is usually a circular walk. Many of these regional or provincial GR trails are charted and waymarked in red-and-yellow by local outdoor organisations such as ABRI (Association Bretonne des Relais et Itineraires) for Brittany, or CHAMINA for the Massif Central. The walker in France will soon become familiar with all these footpath networks, national, regional or local, and find them the perfect way into the heart and heartland of France. As a little bonus, the GR networks are expanding all the time, with the detours — or *varientes* — off the main route eventually linking with other GR paths or *varientes* and becoming GR trails in their own right.

Walkers will find the GR trails generally well marked and easy to follow, and they have two advantages over the footpaths commonly encountered in the UK. First, since they are laid out by local people, they are based on intricate local knowledge of the local sights. If there is a fine view, a mighty castle or a pretty village on your footpath route, your footpath through France will surely lead you to it. Secondly, all French footpaths are usually well provided with a wide range of comfortable country accommodation, and you will discover that the local people, even the farmers, are well used to walkers and greet them with a smile, a '*Bonjour*' and a '*bon route*'.

Terrain arfd Climate

As a glance at these guides or any Topo-guide will indicate, France has a great variety of terrain. France is twice the size of the UK and many natural features are also on a larger scale. There are three main ranges of mountains, the Alps contain the highest mountain in Europe, the Pyrenees go up to 10,000 ft, the Massif Central peaks to over 6000 ft, and there are many similar ranges with hills which overtop our highest British peak, Ben Nevis. On the other hand, the Auvergne and the Jura have marvellous open ridge walking, the Cévennes are steep and rugged, the Ardeche and parts of Provence are hot and wild, the Île de France, Normandy, Brittany and much of Western France is green and pleasant, not given to extremes. There is walking in France for every kind of walker, but given such a choice the wise walker will consider the complications of terrain and weather before setting out, and go suitably equipped.

France enjoys three types of climate: continental, oceanic and mediterranean. South of the Loire it will certainly be hot to very hot from mid-April to late September. Snow can fall on the mountains above 4000 ft from mid-October and last until May, or even lie year-round on the tops and in couloirs; in the high hills an ice-axe is never a frill. I have used one by the Brêche de Roland in the Pyrenees in mid-June.

Wise walkers should study weather maps and forecasts carefully in the week before they leave for France, but can generally expect good weather from May to October, and a wide variety of weather — the severity depending on the terrain — from mid-October to the late Spring.

Accommodation

The walker in France can choose from a wide variety of accommodation with the assurance that the walker will always be welcome. This can range from country hotels to wild mountain pitches, but to stay in comfort, many walkers will travel light and overnight in the comfortable hotels of the *Logis de France* network.

Logis de France: The *Logis de France* is a nationwide network of small, family-run country hotels, offering comfortable accommodation and excellent food. *Logis* hotels are graded and can vary from a simple, one-star establishment, with showers and linoleum, to a four- or five-star *logis* with gastronomic menus and deep-pile carpets. All offer excellent value for money, and since there are over 5000 scattered across the French countryside, they provide a good focus for a walking day. An annual guide to the *Logis* is available from the French Government Tourist Office, 178 Piccadilly, London W1V 0AL, Tel. (01) 491 7622.

Gites d'Etape: A *gîte d'étape* is best imagined as an unmanned youth hostel for outdoor folk of all ages. They lie all along the footpath networks and are usually signposted or listed in the guides. They can be very comfortable, with bunk beds, showers, a well equipped kitchen, and in some cases they have a warden, a *guardien*, who may offer meals. *Gîtes d'étape* are designed exclusively for walkers, climbers, cyclists, cross country skiers or horse-riders. A typical price (1989) would be Fr.25 for one night. *Gîtes d'étape* should not be confused with a *Gîte de France*. A *gîte* — usually signposted as '*Gîte de France*' — is a country cottage available for a holidayt let, though here too, the owner may be more than willing to rent it out as overnight accommodation.

Youth hostels: Curiously enough, there are very few Youth Hostels in France outside the main towns. A full list of the 200 or so available can be obtained from the Youth Hostel Association (YHA), Trevelyan House, St Albans, Herts AL1 2DY.

Pensions or cafes: In the absence of an hotel, a *gîte d'étape* or a youth hostel, all is not lost. France has plenty of accommodation and an enquiry at the village cafe or bar will usually produce a room. The cafe/hotel may have rooms or suggest a nearby pension or a *chambre d'hôte*. Prices start at around Fr.50 for a room, rising to, say, Fr.120. (1989 estimate).

Chambres d'hôte: A *chambre d'hôte* is a guest room or, in English terms, a bed-and-breakfast, usually in a private house. Prices range up from about Fr.60 a night. *Chambres d'hôte* signs are now proliferating in the small villages of France and especially if you can speak a little French are an excellent way to meet the local people. Prices (1989) are from, say, Fr.70 a night for a room, not per person.

Abris: *Abris*, shelters or mountain huts can be found in the mountain regions, where they are often run by the *Club Alpin Francais*, an association for climbers. They range from the comfortable to the primitive, are often crowded and are sometimes reserved for members. Details from the Club Alpin Francais, 7 Rue la Boétie, Paris 75008, France.

Camping: French camp sites are graded from one to five star, but are generally very good at every level, although the facilities naturally vary from one cold tap to shops, bars and heated pools. Walkers should not be deterred by a '*Complet*' (Full) sign on the gate or office window: a walker's small tent will usually fit in somewhere. *Camping à la ferme*, or farm camping, is increasingly popular, more primitive — or less regimented — than the official sites, but widely available and perfectly adequate. Wild camping is officially not permitted in National Parks, but unofficially if you are over 1500m away from a road, one hour's walk from a *gîte* or campsite, and where possible ask permission, you should have no trouble. French country people will always assist the walker to find a pitch.

The law for walkers
The country people of France seem a good deal less concerned about their 'rights' than the average English farmer or landowner. I have never been ordered off land in France or greeted with anything other than friendliness . . . maybe I've been lucky. As a rule, walkers in France are free to roam over all open paths and tracks. No decent

walker will leave gates open, trample crops or break down walls, and taking fruit from gardens or orchards is simply stealing. In some parts of France there are local laws about taking chestnuts, mushrooms (and snails), because these are cash crops. Signs like *Réserve de Chasse*, or *Chasse Privé* indicate that the shooting is reserved for the landowner. As a general rule, behave sensibly and you will be tolerated everywhere, even on private land.

The country code

Walkers in France should obey the *Code du Randonneur*:

- Love and respect Nature.
- Avoid unnecessary noise.
- Destroy nothing.
- Do not leave litter.
- Do not pick flowers or plants.
- Do not disturb wildlife.
- Re-close all gates.
- Protect and preserve the habitat.
- No smoking or fires in the forests. (This rule is essential and is actively enforced by foresters and police.
- Stay on the footpath.
- Respect and understand the country way of life and the country people.
- Think of others as you think of yourself.

Transport

Transportation to and within France is generally excellent. There are no less than nine Channel ports: Dunkirk, Calais, Boulogne, Dieppe, Le Havre, Caen/Ouistreham, Cherbourg, Saint-Malo and Roscoff, and a surprising number of airports served by direct flights from the UK. Although some of the services are seasonal, it is often possible to fly direct to Toulouse, Poitiers, Nantes, Perpignan, Montpellier, indeed to many provincial cities, as well as to Paris and such obvious destinations as Lyon and Nice. Within France the national railway, the SNCF, still retains a nationwide network. Information, tickets and a map can be obtained from the SNCF. France also has a good country bus service and the *gare routière* is often placed just beside the railway station. Be aware though, that many French bus services only operate within the *département*, and they do not generally operate from one provincial city to the next. I cannot encourage people to hitch-hike, which is both illegal and risky, but walkers might consider a taxi for their luggage. Almost every French village has a taxi driver who will happily transport your rucksacks to the next night-stop, fifteen to twenty miles away, for Fr.50 a head or even less.

Money

Walking in France is cheap, but banks are not common in the smaller villages, so carry a certain amount of French money and the rest in traveller's cheques or Eurocheques, which are accepted everywhere.

Clothing and equipment

The amount of clothing and equipment you will need depends on the terrain, the length of the walk, the time of your visit, the accommodation used. Outside the mountain areas it is not necessary to take the full range of camping or backpacking gear. I once walked across France from the Channel to the Camargue along the Grande Randonnée footpaths in March, April and early May and never needed to use any of the camping gear I carried in my rucksack because I found hotels everywhere, even in quite small villages.

Essential items are:
In summer: light boots, a hat, shorts, suncream, lip salve, mosquito repellent, sunglasses, a sweater, a windproof cagoule, a small first-aid kit, a walking stick.
In winter: a change of clothing, stormproof outer garments, gaiters, hat, lip salve, a companion.
In the mountains at any time: large-scale maps (1:25,000), a compass, an ice-axe. In winter, add a companion and ten-point crampons.
At any time: a phrase book, suitable maps, a dictionary, a sense of humour.

The best guide to what to take lies in the likely weather and the terrain. France tends to be informal, so there is no need to carry a jacket or something smart for the evenings. I swear by Rohan clothing, which is light, smart and functional. The three things I would never go without are light, well-broken-in boots and several pairs of loop-stitched socks, and my walking stick.

Health hazards
Health hazards are few. France can be hot in summer, so take a full water-bottle and refill it at every opportunity. A small first-aid kit is sensible, with plasters and 'mole-skin' for blisters, but since prevention is better than cure, loop-stitched socks and flexible boots are better. Any French chemist — a *pharmacie* — is obliged to render first-aid treatment for a small fee. These pharmacies can be found in most villages and large towns and are marked by a green cross.

Dogs are both a nuisance and a hazard. All walkers in France should carry a walking stick to fend off aggressive curs. Rabies — *la rage* — is endemic and anyone bitten must seek immediate medical advice. France also possesses two types of viper, which are common in the hill areas of the south. In fairness, although I found my walking stick indispensable, I must add that in thirty years I have never even seen a snake or a rabid dog. In case of real difficulty, dial 17 for the police and the ambulance.

Food and wine
One of the great advantages with walking in France is that you can end the day with a good meal and not gain an ounce. French country cooking is generally excellent and good value for money, with the price of a four-course menu starting at about Fr.45. The ingredients for the mid-day picnic can be purchased from the village shops and these also sell wine. Camping-Gaz cylinders and cartridges are widely available, as is 2-star petrol for stoves. Avoid naked fires.

Preparation
The secret of a good walk lies in making adequate preparations before you set out. It pays to be fit enough to do the daily distance at the start. Much of the necessary information is contained in this guide, but if you need more, look in guidebooks or outdoor magazines, or ask friends.

The French
I cannot close this introduction without saying a few words about the French, not least because the walker in France is going to meet rather more French people than, say, a motorist will, and may even meet French people who have never met a foreigner before. It does help if the visitor speaks a little French, even if only enough to say '*bonjour*' and '*Merci*' and '*S'il vous plait*'. The French tend to be formal and it pays to be

polite, to say 'hello', to shake hands. I am well aware that relations between France and England have not always been cordial over the last six hundred years or so, but I have never met with hostility of any kind in thirty years of walking through France. Indeed, I have always found that if the visitor is prepared to meet the French halfway, they will come more than halfway to greet him or her in return, and are both friendly and hospitable to the passing stranger.

As a final tip, try smiling. Even in France, or especially in France, a smile and a *'pouvez vous m'aider?'* (Can you help me?) will work wonders. That's my last bit of advice, and all I need do now is wish you *'Bon Route'* and good walking in France.

PAYS DE CAUX AND THE SEINE

by Martin Collins

For a region so close to Britain's shores, Normandy possesses an astonishing diversity of landscape, architecture and tradition – all quintessentially French. Its heartland, as green and pleasant as our own, is renowned for its cheeses, cider and rich cuisine. Outside towns and cities, Normandy's rolling countryside sustains a predominantly agrarian society whose success is manifested in the imposing scale and detail of its domestic buildings. Here and there, smaller enterprises, reluctant to relinquish the old ways, may seem inefficient – even archaic – by today's standards. Yet the patched-up sheds and ruined barns, symbols of an unchanging rural obtuseness, contribute significantly to the country scene. From humble outhouse to the grandest farmstead or town dwelling, the Norman façade is distinguished by an attractive grid of half-timbering.

Normandy is a gastronomic paradise for devotees of French provincial fare and one of the great delights of a walking tour there is savouring regional dishes. Cheeses are legendary, while other specialities in the north of the province include Rouen duck, Caen tripe and Dieppe sole.

With no vineyards of its own, Normandy produces an excellent *cidre* from its prolific apple orchards; the apples, too, are often of fine eating quality. Widely drunk with meals is a between-courses.tot of distilled apple brandy known as *calvados* , whose effects – be warned! – may not be conducive to an early resumption of walking if consumed over lunch!

Up to 30 litres per day of cream-rich milk from each of 5½ million cows forms the mainstay of a large dairy prouducts industry. Despite cream's diminishing popularity in these diet-conscious times, it remains a central ingredient in traditional Norman cuisine.

The western portion of Seine-Maritime *département* is occupied by a distinctive area of undulating chalklands and nowhere on the entire French coast will you find cliffs of such dramatic beauty. Around 8,000 years ago, the north and east of the province were inundated by the sea and deposits of ancient limestone hundreds of metres thick from the ocean bed were laid down. Wind-blown soil rich in organic debris subsequently covered the chalk and prosperous arable and dairy farming has evolved. This is pays de Caux.

Where land meets sea, underlying geology is revealed. So stunning are the chalk cliffs of pays de Caux, striated with flints and yellow marl and riven with hanging valleys, that this is christened the *Côte d'Albarte* – 'Alabaster Coast'. Not unlike the cliffs of Dorset or Sussex, the coastline offers walking of the highest quality. Strenuous at times on 'big dipper' gradients, the GR21 path links resorts from Étretat to Dieppe. Beyond Yport and the commercial port of Fécamp, Petites and Grandes Dalles are tucked into deep wooded combes reminiscent of North Devon. Echoing Étretat's magnificent cliff formations, St. Valéry-en-Caux is flanked by its own walls of chalk. Veules-les-Roses, Sotteville-sur-mer, St. Aubin, Quiberville-Plage, Ste. Marguerite and Pourville-sur-mer, lead on, each with its unique features – colourful fishing boats, seafood stalls, an unspoilt Romanesque church, seaside amenities, military museum.

Dieppe is France's oldest seaside resort. It is also an important port whose origins go back to the Vikings, though much of the existing old town is 18th century. Eminently worth a visit, be sure to see the town centre docks, Grande Rue shopping area and the Château-museum with a good collection of Impressionist paintings.

Although Normandy escaped the fighting of World War I which devastated neighbouring Picardy, it bore the brunt of some of World War II's bitterest combat. It is hard for most of us to invoke images capable of conveying the ferocity of the conflict, particularly following the D-Day landings along the Calvados coast on June 6th 1944. The war remains a recent nightmare for Normandy and the observant walker will notice many signs of its passing, especially on the coast. Commemorative museums, monuments and military cemeteries remind us of those tragic days, though by no means all was lost. As a counterpoint to the savage destruction at Le Havre, Caen and west in the 'bocage', less strategically important areas survived more or less intact.

Inland, pays de Caux's acres of wheat, sugar-beet and flax are punctuated by half-timbered farms, protected by embankments of oak, elm and beech from the prevailing winds and constructed from local flints and stones locked in copious mortar. Water seeps through limestone so the landscape is well drained; water towers, ponds and wells are needed to sustain life. Woods and low ridges and variety to broad horizons, while arabesques of chalk-laden fields in springtime become patchworks of variegated colour and texture as crops mature. Although the land is intensively worked, walking is invigorating beneath big skies.

In places, rivers flow from the Caux plateau west to the sea or south to the Seine. One such is the Durdent which rises near the market town of Yvetot and ends at Veulettes-sur-mer; another the Lézarde from Le Havre to Montivilliers and Étretat.

Pays de Caux is bounded to the south by the River Seine – that most Gallic of rivers, vigorous like a coiled serpent in its lower reaches and for centuries a key to northern France's political and economic security. This vital artery connecting Paris with the sea is a significant natural resource as well as a trading route now that ocean going ships can reach Rouen, 80km upstream. Walking alongside the river's heavy waters gliding west, you sense the open sea 30km away, from the quality of air and reflected light.

Towards its mouth, the Seine is flanked by heavy industry but further inland the valley's great historic buildings echo the chalk outcrops from which they were built – Rouen cathedral, St. Martin-de-Boscherville and the abbey churches of Jumièges and St. Wandrille.

Rouen is Normandy's 'pièce de résistance' for the foreign visitor. Set in a valley beneath wooded hills, it is a city of great antiquity and exhuberance. A long and complex history is revealed through many old buildings, though some were damaged during the war and the marvellous Notre Dame cathedral is still undergoing restoration. With its museums and shopping areas, Rouen is well worth a day's exploration before embarking on one of the walks which begin there.

On the Seine's more interesting northern bank, Duclair is an agreeable town of waterside bars, benches and shady views of river traffic; duck is a local gastronomic speciality. Some compare the mellow ruins of Jumièges Abbey with Fountains or Rievaulx, though its very existence was threatened by careless private ownership until the state acquired the site in 1947.

Across the Seine by ferry lies 17,000 acres of semi-wilderness forest – the Parc Naturel Régional de Brotonne. Protected from development or exploitation, there are few roads and walkers and horse-riders enjoy preferential access.

East of the futuristic Pont de Brotonne stand the elegant abbey ruins of St. Wandrille adjacent to its extraordinary timber-framed monastic church. Almost in Pont de Brotonne's shadow is another charming riverside town – Caudebec-en-Caux – reconstructed in the form of an amphitheatre after severe fire damage in 1940.

Aloof on a wooded spur, Tancarville overlooks its famous suspension bridge which spans the river 20 kilometres upstream from the Atlantic port of Le Havre. The Seine estuary's vast industrial complex rests on alluvial deposits which choked the old ports of Lillebonne and Harfleur.

Le Havre suffered worst than most during the last war and its wholesale reconstruction was orchestrated by Auguste Perret, a contemporary of le Corbusier and a pioneer of reinforced concrete. Hailed at the time as a blueprint from the new modernism and building techniques, the city's grids of grey, monumental buildings seem today impersonal and unyielding.

On a practical note, in pays de Caux few walking routes stray far from human habitation, though not all hamlets or villages possess a shop. During the summer season, refreshments and accommodation are readily obtainable on or near the coast. Buses connect the resorts as well as inland locations, though services should always be verified before being relied upon when planning walks.

Over Seine-Maritime the weather is often fresh and bracing, with temperatures a little higher than in southern England and sunshine hours generous in spring and summer. Rainfall is heaviest in the autumn but unsettled spells can occur at any time. It can become very warm in summer so drinks should be carried in addition to the usual energy rations.

Where walks use farrn tracks and woodland paths, the going is often muddy, requiring stout shoes or boots (even wellington boots for modest distances). Riverside stretches of path are generally more sheltered than on the Caux plateau and coast, but it is advisable to take protective clothing and waterproofs at all times of the year.

By linking sections of GR paths, it is possible to construct many excellent hikes, from a couple of days' duration to upwards of a week, as the following examples show:–

A fine circuit of pays de Caux which samples the best of the coast, countryside and Seine valley, starts at the region's 'capital' – Caudebec-en-Caux (though you could start anywhere on the circuit). Follow the GR2 west and parallel to the Seine to Tancarville and Montivilliers, then turn north on the GR21 to Étretat. The splendid Côte d'Albarte leads you to Veulettes-sur-Mer where the GR211 runs south back to Caudebec.

Also from Caudebec, a good round walk of some 55km begins by following the GR2 westwards to Tancarville, where it crosses the suspension bridge and picks up the GR23 round the low lying Marais Vernier, once a marsh. By flanking the west edge of the Forêt de Brotonne, you arrive opposite Caudebec which is reached by ferry.

A circular hike from Duclair follows the GR23 west to Jumièges, where a ferry crosses the Seine to the Forêt de Brotonne. Stay on GR23 as far as Aizier Ste. Croix then strike north-east along the D65 country road or any 'route forestière' through the forest. Take the ferry to Caudebec-en-Caux and the GR2 east back to Duclair. About 40km.

If spending time at Rouen, it is well worth visiting the *Maison du Tourisme* to obtain details of the many interesting walks in and around the city itself.

WALK 1

ROUEN

Cathedral; several churches with fine carvings; Palais de Justice (Law Courts); Tour Jeanne-d'Arc (Joan of Arc's Tower); many pedestrianised streets; 15th–16th century façades; the Gros Horloge (Great Clock).

The route starts in a suburb of Rouen, Mont-Saint-Aignan, which can be reached by bus from the centre.

MONT-SAINT-AIGNAN

2Km
0:30

The GR25d marking starts at the corner of Maromme Road and Rue Marcel-Dupré. Continue by going left along the Rue Marcel-Dupré, under a road bridge, and then left (west) down into the valley. Walk beside the artificial lake, then turn left onto a path which runs next to the woods and takes you to Notre-Dame-de-Bondeville.

NOTRE-DAME-DE-BONDEVILLE

4Km
1

In Notre-Dame-de-Bondeville turn left onto the D66 and take the first lane to the right, which leads up to the edge of the wood. Turn right onto the path which runs along the edge of the wood; follow this down to the D66 and turn left (north) along it. After 400 metres turn up left onto a footpath through the wood. In front of the forestry house take the D321 left (southwest). At the second crossroads turn right (north-west), onto the footpath which leads you through the forest towards Le Houlme. Go under the railway bridge to reach the N27 on the edge of Le Houlme.

LE HOULME

5.5Km
1:20

In Le Houlme take the N27 to the right, and then turn right into the first lane you reach, which will take you over the railway via a level crossing. At the bend, turn left off the road and go straight up on a path through the wood which then rejoins the road. Go right for a few metres and then continue along the footpath beside the wood. After 1.5 kilometres turn left (north) on to a path which runs between hedges. At La Rue Audière turn left, then immediately right, and follow the road north-east to the D121 in La Ville aux Geais. Take the D121 left for 50 metres, then the footpath

Crossing of two paths

Starting point of link, marked in yellow, through the Verte Wood to join the GR25c at Le Mont-Perreux and Saint-Martin-du-Vivier (10 kilometres).

2Km
0:30

Bois-Isambert

2.5Km
0:40

MONTVILLE

10.5Km
2:35

Le Bout de la Côte

Junction with the GR212 from Sainte-Marguerite.

1.5Km
0:20

right (north-east), leading down to the valley bottom. Turn right there onto the path which takes you into the Saint-Maurice wood. Follow this for 1.5 kilometres until you reach a point where two paths cross.

From the crossing of the paths follow the GR25d left (north) through the small village of Le Bois-le-Vicomte and then along the road in a north-easterly direction past the water-tower to the D47, where there is a coach stop. Take the D47 left for a few metres then turn right down a lane which leads to the hamlet of Bois-Isambert.

At Bois-Isambert take the GR25, which continues westwards through the woods to the market town of Montville.

From the square in Montville take the D155 north, cross the D44, and at the next crossroads follow the road west under the railway bridge. Immediately after the bridge, turn right (north), on to a footpath which goes through undergrowth and then through Le Plix. At the junction (see map IGN ref 160), take the tarmac road to the right, and then after 300 metres take the dirt track to Les Cambres. Follow the road to the left. Cross the N27 and take the dirt track directly opposite. At the second crossing take the footpath left which joins the road at Le Manoir-Bosquet. Turn right along the road, cross the D44 and continue through the hamlets of Val and Tous-Vents. At Tous-Vents turn right. After 250 metres turn left on to a path which goes to the D124. Turn left onto the road and then take the first street on the right, which takes you through Le Bagot and into Le Bagot Wood. When you reach a hollow where three valleys meet, bear northwards through the Le Breuil Wood. The path eventually reaches the D504 on the outskirts of La Cour Souveraine. Take the D504 left (south-west); at the first crossroads turn right onto the road leading to Le Bout de la Côte to join the GR212.

From its junction with the GR212 at Le Bout de la Côte, the GR25 crosses the wood westwards. At the edge of the wood take the path south to meet the D504. Turn right and walk to the junction with the D104 (see map ref 54).

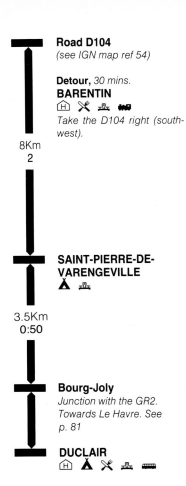

Road D104
(see IGN map ref 54)

Detour, *30 mins.*
BARENTIN
Take the D104 right (south-west).

8Km
2

SAINT-PIERRE-DE-VARENGEVILLE

3.5Km
0:50

Bourg-Joly
Junction with the GR2. Towards Le Havre. See p. 81

DUCLAIR

Keep to the GR25 by taking the D104 eastwards towards Malaunay. After 500 metres turn right on to a dirt track leading under the railway bridge, then up towards the wood and across a road to L'Enfer. From here the path goes south-east until it reaches a road. Follow the road to the right. Cross the N15, which has a coach service to Rouen. Walk beside the Parc d'Esneval and then pass under the A15 motorway at La Cliquette. Keep on until you reach the D67 on the outskirts of Roumare. Follow the D67 to the right for 100 metres, then turn left (south-west), onto a dirt track. When you reach a road, turn right and continue to the crossroads at Le Haridon on the edge of Saint-Pierre-de-Varengeville.

At the crossroads at Le Haridon, turn right, then left. After 200 metres take a dirt track to the right; this brings you on to a lane which passes behind the château. At the next crossroads turn right (north-west), and walk to the edge of the wood. Turn left along a paved path. Cross the D86 and continue straight on to the hamlet of Bourg-Joly, on the western edge of Saint-Pierre-de-Verengeville.

From Bourg-Joly the GR2 (see p. 32–95) will take you to Duclair.

WALK 2

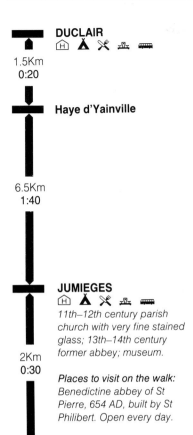

DUCLAIR

1.5Km
0:20

Haye d'Yainville

6.5Km
1:40

JUMIEGES

11th–12th century parish church with very fine stained glass; 13th–14th century former abbey; museum.

2Km
0:30

Places to visit on the walk: Benedictine abbey of St Pierre, 654 AD, built by St Philibert. Open every day.

BAC-DE-JUMIÈGES (Heurteauville)

Junction with the GR23a.

Detour, *visitor information centre. Leave the GR on an unsignposted track, indicated with a dotted line on the map, leading north to an information centre run by the Brotonne Regional Park. Here you will find informative posters, a picnic area, and a*

Keep to the GR2 as it runs south-west from Duclair towards the hamlet of Le Claquemeure. Shortly after it takes you into the forest, you will come to the forest house at Haye d'Yainville and the junction with the GR23a.

To the right (west), the GR2 leads to the village of Le Trait, as marked. Turn south, following the GR23a down through the forest and then along the railway. It will pass underneath the railway and then run around the grounds of the *château* to the hamlet of Saint-Paul. Cross the D982 and continue walking south-east into the forest of Jumièges, passing in front of a chapel and crossing straight over a junction (see map IGN ref 73). At the first crossroads after you come out of the forest, turn left and walk down to the beginning of the Rue Mainberte: turn right on to it and follow it down into Jumièges.

Continue down the street on which you arrived, passing many old houses and the parish church; at the junction with the D143, turn left towards the ruined abbey. There, fork right, still along the D143, and take a path to the right, which will bring you out on a small side road. Turn left and follow the path round to the ferry landing stage at Bac-de-Jumièges.

Pick up the GR23 in front of the Jumièges ferry landing stage. Leave the riverbank and climb up to the left (south-west), following the Val Persil into the Brotonne Forest. Turn right (north), and walk along a woodland path.

panoramic guide at the viewpoint over the Seine.

15Km
4

Lisière de la Forêt
Detour, *10 mins.*

CHOPILLARD
⌂

Go through a gap in the hedge and along the fence which is at right angles to you, until you reach the farm buildings.

Detour
LA HAYE-AUBRÉ
⌂

7Km
2

AIZIER
⛺ ✕

Listed 12th century Norman church.

5Km
1:15

Continuing past the unmarked detour, the route turns westwards to cross the D913. Pass the Chêne Cuvé (an oddly shaped oak tree) and head south-west down into the valley, noting the excavations in the Gallo-Roman ruins. Turn right (north-west), and walk along the valley bottom for 1 kilometre. Then turn left (west), and climb up a steep, narrow path. Cross a forest track; shortly afterwards the path turns south, then west. Cross over several forest roads. The route comes close to the 'Hetre de la Serre' and joins a paved road (see map IGN ref 116).

Turn right (north-west) and walk along the road for 200 metres, before veering left on to a footpath, which crosses a small road and then the D40. Continue until you reach the forest road from La Haye-Aubrée. Turn left (south) along it, and go down to the road from La-Mare-à-La-Chèvre. Cross,and go up again on the opposite side. Cross a forest track; at the top of the hillock (see map IGN ref 106), turn right and walk as far as the road from La Mare aux Anes. Turn left (south) on to this road and, after the first bend, turn right to visit Lisière de la Forêt.

The GR23 route continues along the edge of the wood for 800 metres. Enter the woods and walk along a path which descends in a north-westerly direction into the valley. Follow the valley to the right and, after 400 metres, go up to the left, on a path which leads to a tarmac track. Continue along this to the D131. Cross this road and take the dirt track which swings to the right (due north).

On reaching the forest road from La Mare-à-la-Chèvre, turn left. At the next crossroads continue west along the firebreak, crossing the valley and descending to the D95. Turn left and follow this road to Aizier.

Leave Aizier on the D95 heading south-west. Near the *mairie*, turn left up a lane which goes through Arsault and rejoins the D95. After 100 metres you will reach a fork. Leave the D95 and take a path to the left leading to Le Manoir de Thorold. Cross the D95 again on the outskirts of Le Vieux-Port, and take the rural track which runs along the Seine. Pass the

former lighthouse and, a little further on, after passing one path, take the second path, to the left which goes through the wood to Le Bout-Deshayes.

LE BOUT-DESHAYES

2Km
0:30

At Le Bout-Deshayes, take the small road to the right (north-west), cross the D89, and continue along the tarmac road, which is almost immediately opposite the crossing point and heads south-west to Le Carrefour. Cross over the D179 via the bridge and join the N182 road.

Road N182
Detour, *15 mins.*
SAINTE-OPPORTUNE-LA-MARE

1Km
0:15

Follow the N182 going south.

Cross the N182 and walk down into the La Mar Wood until you reach a road. Follow this to the crossroads (see map IGN ref 12) at La Vallée.

La Vallée
Waterfowl breeding centre; experimental centre for introducing Scottish cattle to local conditions.

5.5Km
1:30

At these crossroads, turn left along the road for 2 kilometres, passing through Le Quai de la Forge. After a while, at a fork, turn left on to a dirt track which leads up towards the wood. At the first junction, veer right, cross a road and continue up to the D90. Turn right (west), along this road until you reach the church at Bouquelon.

BOUQUELON
Viewpoint over Le Marais-Vernier, Seine estuary, and Tancarville bridge.

5Km
1:15

At Bouquelon church leave the D90 and take a street which runs south-west between houses. At the crossroads before Le Clos Beauvais, turn right (north). At the next crossroads take the path directly ahead of you. This passes through the undergrowth and reaches a road. Turn right; after 100 metres turn left on to a track, which brings you to a tarmac road. Turn left (north-west) and follow the road to the village of Marais-Vernier.

MARAIS-VERNIER
Many old cottages.

2.5Km
0:40

From here, follow a road along the hillside, turning left after a while and then right. At Le Bout-d'Aval take the path which goes left up through the wood; at the top turn right on to the road to Le Castel.

LE CASTEL

Go through Le Castel. At the second crossroads, you cross the D711. Continue to the left (westwards) on a footpath which leads down to the Grandes Roques path. Turn right (north) along it, passing close to the former lighthouse

at Pointe de la Roque. Continue across the N178 to the Seine at Feu de l'Épi. Turn right (north-east), and walk beside the Seine until you reach a road which runs parallel to the bridge. Follow this to the right (south-east), rejoin the N178, and cross the Seine by the Tancarville Bridge, from where there is a panoramic view. After the tollgate follow the D910 and at the fork, by the statue of the Virgin, bear right to the church at Tancarville.

12Km
3

TANCARVILLE

🏠 ✗ ⚓ 🚃

Junction with GR2.
12th–14th century castle;
suspension bridge.

WALK 3

TRIEL-SUR-SEINE

🏠 ✕ 🍷 🚊 🚌

Small town attractively located on the right bank of the Seine at the edge of the Hautil plateau. Church, combining Gothic and Renaissance styles with 12th century façade, 16th century south porch, 16th century stained-glass windows by Jean le Prince.

5.9Km
1:30

Chemin Départemental 14E2

Minor road with little traffic, from Vaux-sur-Seine to Boisemont.

Detour, *from Chemin*
2.4Km *Départemental 14E2 to*
0:40 *Vaux-sur-Seine (unmarked)*

On leaving the station turn right down the street beside the railway. At the second bridge turn right and walk up the Rue Galande. (To the left, the street descends, passing below the church.) After a steep climb, turn left into the Rue des Bois and pass the cemetery. Where it ends turn right, passing several small blocks of flats on the way to a crossroads. Turn left into the Grande Sente des Beaux-Regards, on the hillside, with views over the Seine and its valley. At the beginning of a downward slope, fork right onto a track through the woods; 1 kilometre further on, take a path to the left, which leads down to a stone-paved path. Follow this first to the right, then shortly afterwards to the left. Walk along the edge of a field until you reach another path; turn right along it (at Port-Maron). Cross a kind of broad track, the result of underground quarrying, and continue across a level stretch of ground. After passing a tunnel, which can be seen to the right, turn left at the fork and descend slightly. At the next fork the track on the left descends towards Vaux-sur-Seine, but you continue straight on. After a while the route curves right on the Chemin des Petites-Carrières and climbs up the side of a small valley which lies below to the left. Cross a small wood, then loop down to the left. After 200 metres of tarred road turn right, up the Rue du Temple at the bottom of the valley. Pass a small factory on the left, and follow the track as it bends left. The route reaches the plateau, almost immediately passes a rubbish tip and turns right. This brings you to the Chemin Départemental 14E2.

To reach the station at Vaux-sur-Seine go down the small road to the left for 1 kilometre, then bear left on another road which crosses over the railway line. You can see the station 100 metres further on to the left. To return to the GR, turn right as you leave the station. Cross the bridge over the railway lines and continue straight on up. Turn right along the second street you come to, which zig-zags upwards. After about 700 metres it reaches the GR2: right towards Triel, left towards Evecquemont.

Cross the D14E2, then a small wood and some fields. Pass the Château of Fort-Vache, to your left, then on the right a small, disused plaster works. Carry straight on, crossing a small road and some more fields. Go down slightly and at a fork in a small wood bear left. This soon brings you to the outskirts of Évecquemont.

ÉVECQUEMONT
Ⓨ
Fortified 13th century church, restored in 16th century.

Go right through the village, keeping in roughly the same direction. The route takes you past the front of the church, then down past the cemetery. The tarred road you are following soon turns left while the GR, at the beginning of the bend, goes straight on up a very short steep climb through a copse. Cross the D922 (previously the N322) and continue along a good paved track, which at first runs between orchards and small fields. After passing a wood on the right you come out above the valley of the Aubette where there is a panoramic view encompassing the slopes of Meulan on the left, Tessancourt-sur-Aubette below, and as a backdrop, the slopes and woods of Gaillon, Jambville, and Galluis. Take the good paved track down towards the valley passing between fields, orchards and hedges. There are good picnic places here. When the track veers to the right, within view of a half-buried water-tower, turn left along a less frequented track between hedges which comes out on to a flat paved road above Tessancourt.

3.5Km
0:50

MEULAN
Ⓗ ✕ Ⓨ 🚃 🚌
On leaving station small GR2 diversion goes right to Oinville.

Alternative route *(to join the GR from Meulan)*: Meulan to Junction of GR1 and GR2. Pick up the GR1 diversion by walking left down the station avenue and bearing left on the Boulevard Carnot, which is an extension of the Rue G.-Clemenceau. Continue straight on up the Rue de la Chaine and turn off it to the left, heading for the Saint-Nicolas slope. On reaching the church, go round it to the left, noting the view over the town and the valley of the Seine. Near the east end of the church, climb up some stone steps to the left, then walk along the Sainte-Avoie Lane between the old walls. This lane bears left and then down to the Rue des Carrières; turn right along this for 50 metres. Go up the Impasse des Réservoirs to the right, then left past the cemetery. Walk down again, left, to open ground, first beside the cemetery wall and then bearing right between bushes. Pass a copse and a housing estate and go

2.7Km
0:45

down to the left, via the Allée des Ibis, followed by the Allée de l'Ile-de-France until you reach a crossroads. Leaving Meulan directly behind you, turn towards the north-east and follow a small street with access restricted to riverside inhabitants. Take the pedestrian tunnel under the main road (D922) and pick up the street heading north-east which turns into a road above the Aubette. At the fork, leave the Chemin des Petites Fontaines on your left and carry on along the paved road, still heading north-east. You come to the junction of the GR1 and the GR2 within sight of Tessancourt-sur-Aubette; the GR1 continues straight on, north-east, towards Us, while the GR2 bears left, north-west, to Tessancourt; to the right, south-east, the GR1 and GR2 head towards Triel.

Junction of GR1 and GR2

The GR2 crosses a small road and continues straight down the Évecquemont footpath, which turns into a street lined with houses, the beginnings of Tessancourt-sur-Aubette.

TESSANCOURT-SUR-AUBETTE

Recently restored 12th century church.

Carry on, in the same direction, along the Petites Fontaines track which crosses the valley bottom and over a bridge before ascending towards the church. Walk round the church to the right and up to the D28. Cross this road and continue straight on along the Gaillon track, which soon reaches the base of a retaining wall.

Turn left at the retaining wall and climb up to the plateau, coming out by a ruined barn. From here, there is a fine view. Continue along the dirt track in the same direction, despite the absence of marking posts. Towards the centre of the plateau the path crosses a dirt track heading almost north-south, which follows the path of a Roman way called the 'Chaussée Brunehaut'. Do not veer right on the plateau but keep towards the edge of the valley, which soon falls away to the left. Finally, go down past a clump of pine trees, leaving them to your left. Turn left, and then immediately right on to a small tarred road which soon brings you to Gaillon.

2.4Km
0:40

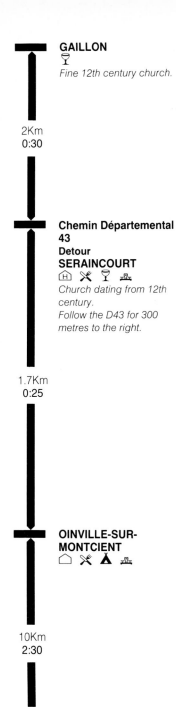

GAILLON
Fine 12th century church.

2Km
0:30

Chemin Départemental 43
Detour
SERAINCOURT
Church dating from 12th century.
Follow the D43 for 300 metres to the right.

1.7Km
0:25

OINVILLE-SUR-MONTCIENT

10Km
2:30

Find the square and, with your back to the church, take the Grande-Rue to the right, then immediately turn up left on the Chemin de la Cavé. This takes you along the park wall of Gaillon Château and brings you to a cross-roads by a large farm on the left. Carry on, in the same direction, on a footpath between a long meadow on the left and a wood on the right. A bit further on, walk through the wood, then turn left on to a path which descends steeply at first, with three sharp bends, and then more gently. It comes out into fields and meets the Chemin Départemental 43.

Follow the D43 to the left for a few metres, then turn right on to the small road beside La Bernon stream, which is on the right behind a wire fence. Beyond the old mill buildings, turn left on to a slightly sunken path. Once you are on the plateau veer gradually to the right, following a power line which ends near an isolated hut. About 200 metres further on, at a junction beside a house, take a right-angled left turn (not waymarked). Go down again, following a good paved path which bears slightly to the right before coming to the bottom of the Moncient valley, where you come to the D913 (formerly the N313) and the outlying houses of Oinville-sur-Montcient.

Cross the D913, bearing a little to the left. Turn immediately right into the Rue de Gournay, pass a small factory, and continue into the heart of the village. Pass the driveway entrance to the *Auberge de Jeunesse* (Youth Hostel) on the left, then turn left and walk to the cross-roads. Turn left there, and continue until you are just past the church; turn right into a street going up between a meadow and some houses. Continue up a sunken pathway, beside some telephone lines, which turns left and emerges on to the plateau. You soon reach a junction in an open field, near pylons carrying a high tension cable; this marks the

6Km
1:30

MEULAN-HARDRICOURT STATION

beginning of the diversion linking Oinville-sur-Moncient with the railway station at Meulan-Hardricourt.

Alternative route Oinville-sur-Moncient to the railway station at Meulan-Hardricourt. Continue along the sunken path by the telephone lines until you reach a water reservoir. Bear right on the path there, crossing fields and going through a copse. Veer left as you come out of the trees. At the next fork take the path to the left (which is often very muddy) through the wood. When it comes out in the corner of a field, carry straight on beside the wood. When you come to the end of the wood, follow the dirt track for about 1.5 kilometres across the open field, keeping in roughly the same direction. There is no waymarking.

When you come to a small tarred road turn right down it, pass a water reservoir, and take the first path on the right. After the cemetery, enter the wood, taking the first path on the left. The route leads to a château and turns left down to the church at Hardricourt, on the right. Circle the church to the left and continue down, under the railway bridge, and immediately up to the left to the railway station at Meulan-Hardricourt, on the Paris–Saint-Lazare line.

To return to the GR2 at Oinville, come out of the station and turn right down the ramp beside the railway line. Go under the bridge and take the road on the left bearing up to the church at Hardricourt. Go round the church to the right. In front of it take a path to the right which runs between woods and meadows. On the edge of the wood turn right, pass the cemetery, turn left up a small, sunken tarred road, and walk past the reservoir to the edge of the plateau. Instead of going straight on, take the dirt track which bears left through the fields. It is not waymarked for about 1.5 kilometres, but keep walking in the same direction to the corner of a wood, then walk along the edge of the wood. Ignore the first path on the right and the next one to the left before taking a path through the wood. Continue between a field on the left and a wood to the right, which you soon enter. This brings you out into fields and to a reservoir. Take the path on the left, following a telephone line to

the first crossing, beside a high tension cable. Here you pick up the GR2 marking: straight on to Oinville and Triel, or left to Limay.

While the Meulan diversion goes straight on, the GR2 turns right on a dirt track between two pylons carrying a high tension line. This brings you to a second dirt track; turn right on to it, then left off it after 12 metres. There are very few route markings here. Take a third dirt track, in poor condition, up towards a group of apple trees. A path on the left takes you into a wood and gently upwards. At the first junction turn right; at the next three crossings turn successively left, right, and then left again. Then, after bearing right at a fork, you reach a small tarred road from Juziers to La Chartre.

Detour, *2.5Km to the railway station at Juziers. Turn left here.*

Turn right on to this road and go under the high tension wires to reach a large clearing on the left of the road. When the road bends to the right, turn left off it on to a path which leads into the La Croix de la Chartre wood, and is often very muddy. Watch where you step as vipers have been found in the wood. After about 1 kilometre, you will come to a fork; bear right along the fence of a television relay station. Cross the D130 and carry straight on along a public path between two privately-owned woods; do not leave the path. Carry on in the same direction until you reach the tarred road from Guitrancourt to Brueil-en-Vexin; on the right there is a panoramic view over the Montcient valley and the wooded hillsides overlooking it. Continue down the road to the left. You will soon have an extensive view over the Seine valley, which unfortunately is heavily industrialised. After about 1 kilometre the road meets a good-quality dirt track. Turn right along it. There is very little waymarking where it begins. Continue, with very little change of direction, across fields and orchards to the outskirts of Fontenay-Saint-Père.

6Km
1:30

FONTENAY-SAINT-PÈRE
♈ 🚂

Walk right through the village, which is very spread out, keeping in roughly the same direction and taking first the Rue de l'Ancienne-Mairie, then the Rue de la Mairie, and then the Rue Pasteur. The route takes you towards a beautiful church, and comes out into the square. Continue for a short distance along the Rue Pasteur, pass the church and bear left

4Km
1

Follainville
Public wash-house on Rue des Lavoirs.

Detour, *short cut to Mantes route*

into the Rue de Mantes. This leads downhill, out of the village, and then up again as far as the N183 road. Turn left along this for 50 metres. Next, turn right on to a paved road by the park wall of Le Mesnil Château, and enter the wood. One kilometre after leaving the N183 you reach a roundabout, with surrounding walls and a big gate to the right of it.

The GR2 continues slightly to the left. After 1.2 kilometres it emerges from the wood and bears left on a good paved road which, under the name of Rue du Bois, soon reaches Follainville.

Continue along the Rue du Bois to its junction with the Rue Jules-Ferry, and turn right along this road.

Detour, see left. By turning left to the Rue Jules-Ferry and then bearing right on the Rue A.-France, you reach the Place du Mesnil. Cross this, going slightly uphill, and turn immediately right into the Rue du Maloret, which then becomes a dirt track rejoining the Mantes detour. This route is marked in yellow, and provides a short cut to the Mantes route.

The GR2 itself turns right, passes in front of the *mairie*, bears right to go down the Rue Wilson past the lovely old church, and soon turns right again into the first street, Rue Pasteur. (If you continue a little further you come to the Rue des Lavoirs and the fine public wash house.) Walk down the Rue Pasteur, which ends at the Mantes detour which comes in from the left.

Alternative route Follainville Mantes-la-Jolie and Limay Walk up the Rue Saint-Martin, turn left on to the tarred road for a few metres, then climb up a narrow footpath through the wood, which leads to a wider path. Turn right here and continue through the wood. When the path emerges, it bends left and goes uphill. Before you get to a water reservoir and some houses, which you can see up ahead, turn right on to a good quality path between hedges. Turn right off this after 300 metres on to an erratic track between bushes and clumps of trees which leads to the edge of the plateau and then down into the valley. The track soon goes back into the wood, climbing past a spring and

coming out near a clump of pine trees, from where there is an extensive view over the valley. Continue along another good footpath down the hillside; this becomes the Saint-Sauveur path through the houses on the edge of Limay. Go down a steep little path to the right, across a road, and down a second steep path. Then turn right along the road and, shortly afterwards, turn left on to a path, which leads to the Seine. Walk along the river to the Limay bridge, where you meet the GR11 coming in from Magny-en-Vexin.

7Km
1:45

To reach the railway station at Mantes-la-Jolie, go straight along the main road, turn right into the wide Avenue de la République, then left into the Rue du Président-Roosevelt, which is not way-marked. For the Mantes Station, which is nearer but not a stop for the through trains to Paris, bear left slightly towards the Church of Notre-Dame along the Rue Thiers. Then take the Rue de la Porte-aux-Saints and the Boulevard V.-Duhamel. All go in roughly the same direction and are marked GR11.

MANTES-LA-JOLIE
Ⓗ ✗ Ⱥ ⚓ ⛟ ⛟ ℹ

12th–13th century church of Notre Dame; 16th century Saint-Maclou tower; 12th–13th century church at Gassicourt where the famous 17th century preacher and writer Bossuet was Prior.

To reach Follainville, leave the station at Mantes-la-Jolie, turn right along the Avenue du Président-Roosevelt, bear right into the wide Avenue de la République, and then left into the Rue Nationale as far as the bridge (not way-marked). Coming out of Mantes Station, take the Boulevard Victor-Duhamel, the Rue Porte-aux-Saints, then the Rue Thiers, go past the church of Notre Dame, and cross the Seine via the Limay bridge (GR11 markings) into Limay.

LIMAY
Ⓗ ✗ ⛟ ⚓

12th–16th century church of Saint-Aubin; ruins of the 12th–15th century Vieux-Pont (the Old Bridge).

After crossing the bridge at Limay, leave the GR11 which continues straight on towards Magny-en-Vexin. The GR2 detour goes down left and follows the banks of the Seine, going westward. After 1.5 kilometres turn right on to a path between some houses, then right on to a road. Climb up a steep path to the Saint-Sauveur path, which is tarred, and turn left along it, past some fine houses. From here, and for some distance, there are magnificent contrasting views of the meadows along the Seine, the woods and fields, and large townscapes; and also between the magnificent collegiate church at Mantes and the smoky factories. Once past the houses the path climbs up fairly steeply. Continue in roughly

1.5Km
0:30

the same direction, passing under overhanging rocks (danger to the right). Cross a small well-situated clump of pine trees to reach the edge of the plateau. Here the path plunges into the wood and zig-zags down, passing close to the Saint-Sauveur spring, to come out into rough clear ground. Now, climb back up to the edge of the plateau through bushes and thorn hedges. The path may be overgrown or even completely hidden, but by following it you soon come to a fine grassy track. Turn left here, and after 300 metres, surrounded by fields and hedges, this takes you to another larger paved path. On the right you can see the new houses on the edge of Follainville-Dennemont, and a high water reservoir. Turn left on to a paved path which runs gently downhill, passing a wood on the edge of the plateau, and then bearing right. It will take you into Haut-de-Dennemont Wood and then continues to the corner of a field on the left.

Detour *By following the yellow markings straight ahead, you can rejoin the GR2 as it enters Follainville. Here you can either take an interesting detour into the village, by turning towards Bonnières, or go back to Triel (it is 26 kilometres from the station at Mantes to the station at Bonnières by this route).*

The route you have been following now bears left and continues down a narrow track through the trees to reach an asphalt road heading to Follainville. Without going into the village, follow the road for a few metres to the left, then walk down the Rue Saint-Martin to the end, where you meet the GR2. Go straight on for Bonnières or Vernon.

At the bottom of the Rue Pasteur bear slightly to the right. Go between a large farm on the right and a strange very low stone cross, then straight up the other side of the hill on a dirt track. At the top enter the wood to your left, on a winding footpath which takes you down to Coudray. Go through this hamlet, past the fire hydrant, and then close to a riding club, on a small road which goes gently uphill. After an old stone cross take the second dirt track to the right. There is a sign indicating 'Chemin de la Messe'. This track takes you gently up to a sort of pass. It is worth climbing up to the left on to the Hurtrel Hillock, a disused claypit containing large lumps of flint nodules, from

where there is an extensive view over a loop of the Seine. The GR continues straight down, past an old stone cross, which is slightly hidden beside an orchard, on to a path called the Chemin de Charielle and into the village of Saint-Martin-la-Garenne.

SAINT-MARTIN-LA-GARENNE
✗ ᵂ ⚓
Church with Norman bell-tower.

3Km
0:45

Near a concrete fountain take the small road up to the right, towards La Désirée Farm and Le Chenay wood. There are two fine views over the cliffs of the Seine towards Vétheuil and La Roche-Guyon, before you come to an attractive 2-kilometre walk through the woods. These woods are mostly private, but walkers are allowed to take the path through them, in spite of any indication to the contrary. The path leaves the wood, giving a beautiful view over Vétheuil and the cliffs, and descends to the outskirts of Vétheuil.

VÉTHEUIL
🏠 ✗ ᵂ ⚓ 🚌
Fine 12th century church, with two magnificent carved doors, and very old statues — provided inspiration for several Impressionist painters, including Monet.

Detour *Yellow markings off to the right of the church square indicate the route of the local Follainville and Vétheuil footpath circuit, the latter coming back to the Place de la Mairie. (See the local footpath guide for further details.)*

8.7Km
2

Continue via the D147 and the Rue de Bourg, coming from Limay, as far as the small square, where the church can be seen on the left, in its magnificent terrace setting. Approach it along the Rue Claude-Monet and then up some old steps.

Pass to the left of the terrace in front of the church, then go up the path beside the cemetery. At the fork, where there is a cross, take the Chérence path to the left, and follow the best of the tracks leading to the top of a steep slope. The GR2 now runs along the hillside to La Roche-Guyon, sometimes just on the edge of the plateau and sometimes below it, but always with an extensive view over the Seine and the Forest of Moisson on the opposite bank. Unfortunately, the latter is marred by intrusive gravel diggings. Follow the route along the edge of the plateau for the first 4 kilometres, varying between dirt tracks, small paths, and more or less distinguishable foot-paths with rather irregular waymarking. The sloping ground to the left is a mixture of woods, cleared ground, and undergrowth. Walkers may enjoy exploring this area on erratic paths which sometimes descend to the clifftops and chalky peaks, visible from far away. However, watch your footing, it may be slippery, and therefore dangerous in wet

weather. On the right you will see fields, the Chérence gliding station (no admittance) and then fields again. Finally, near the edge of the wood, but still within it, there is a well marked path which comes out opposite an isolated house and joins a good paved path. Turn left along it and walk down to a sharp bend.

Detour
Haute-Isle and the D913
Continue down this path if you are going to the village of Haute-Isle and the D913. There are several cave-dwellings here; in particular, by following the main road for another 100 metres towards Vétheuil, you come to a strange church (1670) cut into the chalk, with only its small belfry showing out of the cliff. Visits only by pre-arrangement with the mayor. The 17th century classic writer Boileau often stayed in Haute-Isle with his nephew, who was probably responsible for creating the church.

Leave the paved road at the bend and take a narrow footpath to the right which twists between the bushes up to the edge of the plateau. Continue on through clearings and copses. After a while, the path goes down again slightly, and then continues along the hillside, round several grassy knolls from where one can see La Roche-Guyon, and between fences. In front of a new water tower, cross a small, steep tarred road and, 10 metres lower down, take a good path to the right. This leads through the wood, above the church and the château. Above, perched on the clifftop, are the dominating ruins of the castle keep. Finally, you come to a set of steps which brings you out between the church and the château fence. Walk along the fence to reach the centre of La Roche-Guyon.

LA ROCHE-GUYON
🏠 ✕ 🍷 🚉 🚌
Donjon ruins of castle; 12th century château, lived in by François I, and La Rochefoucauld who wrote part of his Maxims here, also Rommel's headquarters in 1944; 18th century market hall; Louis XV fountain; beautiful shady walk along banks of Seine.

2.7Km
0:45

Take the D913 past the château gate and wall. Turn right into the Rue de la Glacière, then right again into a street which immediately upwards to the left. Pass the remains of several cave dwellings and come out on to a broad ridge. Take the D100, known as the Route des Cretes (the Hill Top Road) to the left, cross the D913 on to a good paved track directly opposite. There are fine viewpoints: left over the Seine valley, right over the green Epte valley. After passing an underground reservoir the track brings you to the Chemin Vicinal Ordinaire, the small tarred road between Clachaloze and Gommecourt.

Chemin Vicinal Ordinaire
Detour
Bonnières (see p. 55)

Bonnières (see p. 55)

From here, you can take a detour which leads to Bonnières station. Cross the road and continue straight ahead on a pleasant dirt track between cleared ground, old orchards and clumps of trees; this area is unfortunately popular with Sunday cross-country motor-cyclists. Keeping in the same direction, enter

5Km
1:30

BONNIÈRES
ⓗ ✗ ♨ 🚍 🚃

5Km
1:30

the wood via a fine avenue. At the corner of a plantation of apple trees, turn left and leave the wood, going downwards on a good paved track. Cross a tarred road and continue on a grass track beside pastureland. Cross a path and continue in roughly the same direction until you reach a good paved track. Turn right along this, at the corner of a small thicket. The track crosses fields and orchards, always in the same general direction, to the junction of five roads. Take the first tarred road to the left; this is the Rue du Temple which soon descends between the outlying houses of Gloton (the hamlet of Bennecourt). Where it turns left, take the Rue de la Charrière to the right, down to the path along the bank of the Seine. Turn left, cross the bridges and, immediately on the other side, turn left along the river, walking down the Promenade Marie-Guillet, which is lined with fine trees. Continue in this direction until you reach Bonnières station, via a tunnel under the railway line.

To join the GR2, leave the station and find the first waymarking on the left. Go under the railway line, turn immediately left and walk along the Promenade Marie-Guillet until you reach a slope leading to the bridge over the Seine. Cross the two branches of the river, then turn right into the hamlet of Gloton. Soon afterwards, turn left, by a *boucherie-charcuterie* (butcher's & delicatessen), into the Rue de la Charrière which climbs up between the houses, bends to the right, and reaches a small tarred road, the Rue du Temple. Go up this to the left. When you reach the plateau, there is a junction of five ways; take the first paved road on the right, which runs between orchards. After about 1 kilometre, at the top of the slope down to Tripleval and at the corner of a thicket, turn left on to a grass track and first cross a field track, then a tarred road. After this, return to the plateau via a good paved track, which comes to some woods. Take the second track to the right, just past a plantation of apple trees, for a pleasant stroll through woods, then across cleared ground, old orchards and clumps of trees, with fine views to the left over the Epte valley and to the right, after climbing a little, glimpses of the Seine. Soon the track brings you to a small road which leads to a crossroads, where you will find the GR2

1.2Km
0:20

GOMMECOURT
🍷 ⛴

1Km
0:15

SAINTE-GENEVIÈVE-LÈS-GASNY
🚌

Detour *1.7Km*
GASNY
🏠 ✕ ⛴
Turn right along the D5.

Detour: *This is the beginning of an attractive circuit, more or less following the top of the slope, to Manitaux, 2 kilometres from Vernonnet. There are continuous fine views, first over the Epte valley, then the Seine valley.*

4.8Km
1:30

waymarking: straight on to Limay, left for Vernon.

Coming from Limay the Bonnières detour continues straight ahead and the GR2 turns right, down the small tarred road, which leads into the Rue des Écoles taking you into Gommecourt.

Continue in the same direction, along the Grande-Rue which crosses through the village. Descend to the valley bottom via a small road which crosses several branches of the Epte. Keep an eye out for the paddle wheels of two old mills which should be visible to the left. Continue on to Sainte-Geneviève-lès-Gasny.

Cross the D5 and go straight along the small tarred road. Turn left off it on to a tarred track which soon goes uphill. Leave it for a paved track up to the right. After some hairpin bends, the track runs between very steep banks. Ignore a private path going off towards fields on the left and continue climbing. The path eventually reaches the plateau, coming out into fields surrounded by woods, and continues in the same direction. When you come to a barrier preventing access to the forest, turn left. This new path soon brings you to the top of the Epte valley.

The GR goes down to the left. Shortly after passing an electricity line it turns right on to a well made, attractive footpath which runs along the hillside between bushes. It curves and climbs slightly to the right, winding through a small wood, then descending gently through another wood, where you will find large numbers of wild orchids in May. At the bottom of the valley cross a path (which to the left leads to the small nearby hamlet of Falaise), then climb up again for a short way, leave the wood, and continue on along the hillside. After another slight descent through bushes, go under a high tension wire to a field. Cross it, walking downhill, then take the first track you come to which is wide enough for use by vehicles. This brings you close to the first houses in Giverny.

GIVERNY

✕ ⛽ 🚌

*House and gardens of
Impressionist painter Claude
Monet (open to the public).*

**4.8Km
1:15**

VERNON

Ⓗ ⌂ ⛺ ✕ 🍷
⛽ 🚍 🚌

*14th century church of Notre
Dame (origin of Monet's
series of cathedral
paintings); Archives Tower
(heavily restored remains of
1123 castle keep). Junction*

The GR avoids the D5; after twisting between houses it joins the Blanche-Hoschédé-Monet path on which you turn right; Monet's house is very close by on the left. Walk up this track to a small square above the school-house/*mairie*. Turn up to the right for 100 metres on a small tarred road, then left on to a footpath which climbs steeply up to a dirt track. Turn left and follow it along a ledge above the outskirts of Giverny. Then go down a short but steep hill via another path which runs between two hedges. Take the first good track to the right, also between hedges, which brings you gently back to the hilltop. Turn left on the plateau, on to a broad grassy track which soon narrows and takes you briefly into the woods before coming out at the first good viewpoint on this section of the GR2. A few metres before the viewpoint the GR starts to go steeply down to the right on a narrow footpath through the trees. It turns right past the fence of a military area, which occupies the plateau and its south-west slope as far as Vernonnet, then reaches the hamlet of Manitaux. Just before you reach the hamlet's first house, on a bend, leave the track to the right to take a narrow path between a big sweet chestnut tree and the military fence. After about 100 metres through the bushes, take the Sentier des Hautes-Eaux to the right, with the disused railway track running parallel below it. This gives you an easy walk to Vernonnet, entering the village as a narrow footpath between garden walls. You come out in front of a restaurant in the Rue de la Ravine; turn left and continue to the end of the road, by the Seine. Go up the Rue de l'Île-de-l'Horloge to the right, which soon brings you to Vernon bridge. From the bridge there is a panoramic view of the river banks, the church of Notre Dame, the Château des Tournelles and the two forests framing the town.

with branch of GR26, Paris–Vernon–Deauville.

Detour: *20 mins, 1.3Km Vernonnet to Vernon station*

5.5Km
1:25

Cross the bridge and carry straight on along the Rue d'Albuféra; a very short detour to the left down the Rue Carnot gives you a view of the church and some 15th century houses. The Rue d'Albuféra brings you directly to the railway line, where you turn right into the Rue de la Gare, close by the station.

To walk from Vernon station to the GR2: On leaving the station turn immediately right beside the railway line, then turn into the Rue d'Albuféra, the first street on the left. Walk straight through the town to the bridge, and cross over it. For Les Andelys: bear left. For Limay: go down the Rue de l'Ile-de-l'Horloge to the right and along the Seine. Turn left into the first street, Rue de la Ravine, cross the D5 and then take a lane to the right, opposite a restaurant.

Without crossing the bridge the GR bears up to the right along an avenue of lime trees, passes the front of the Centre Municipal de Jeunesse des Tourelles, and then, 150 metres further on, takes the Rue Pierre-Bonnard. Turn into the first street on the right to reach the Rue des Pénitents; turn right along this street, then take the Rue du Docteur-Chanoine to the left. Cross the D181, stay on the D313 (formerly the N313) for 50 metres, and turn right into the Chemin de la Justice, which is tarred at first and then paved, and climbs steeply. Walk under two high tension lines. There is a fine view back over Vernon and the Seine valley. At the top of the slope the GR enters the Vernon forest. N.B. This is privately owned, so keep to the track, which is a public right of way. Continue almost straight on for a kilometre. After crossing a clearing, leave the forest house of Le Clos-Cerqueux on your right and walk under some very large trees to a cross-roads. Keep walking straight ahead, still on a broad forest avenue. One kilometre beyond the crossing, after passing through another clearing, there is the stump of an old oak tree on the left, 'La Mère de Dieu' (Mother of God) tree, with a statue of the Virgin and offerings. About 500 metres further on, there is a forest house on the right (see map IGN ref 127). One kilometre beyond this house the path leaves the wood and continues on towards the plain and the D117 road. Follow this for 30 metres until you come to the first house in Panilleuse.

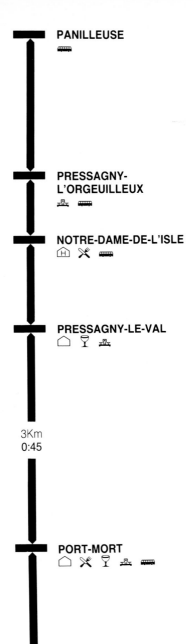

PANILLEUSE

Without going into the village the GR2 turns left at La Malira farm, on to a small road heading towards Corville. At the end of the farm wall turn left (south-west), towards the forest of Vernon, following a route shared with a local walk marked in yellow. The GR descends into the Courbe Valley. Turn right, by a cross, on to the road to Val. Further on turn left along a track and then take the Rue de la Marette, left, into Pressagny-l'Orgeuilleux.

PRESSAGNY-L'ORGEUILLEUX

Cross the D313, leaving the church on your left. Before reaching the Seine turn right (north-west) into the Pieds-Corbons path which leads to Notre-Dame-de-l'Isle.

NOTRE-DAME-DE-L'ISLE

Take the Rue Maurice-Coeuret, then the Rue Léopold-Joly. In front of Le Mesnil farm turn right on to a grass track and walk to the D313. Turn right along this for a few metres. Then turn left on to a dirt track beside a stretch of water. A road brings you into Pressagny-le-Val.

PRESSAGNY-LE-VAL

The GR2 follows the Rue Georges-Clergeot and, beyond the church, turns left into the Rue du Sergent-Henri-Seney. Pass the public washhouse which faces the bar-grocery. Leave the village via the Rue Lucien-Lefrançois to the left. This becomes the VO104 road. About 300 metres beyond the last house in the village the GR2 turns right on to a dirt track with a view of the Seine, which is very wide at this point. Follow this track, for roughly 400 metres, to a large hedge; turn left beside this hedge, following a narrow pathway downhill. Before reaching the road, turn right along a good dirt track between two fields; there is very little waymarking. One kilometre along here you pass La Mi-Voie (half-way).

3Km
0:45

PORT-MORT

Carry straight on across the fields for about 1.2 kilometres. Having crossed several tracks the GR reaches the hamlet of Port-Mort, on the edge of La Falaise. The route enters Rue des Vignes, bears slightly to the right then to the left, narrows and crosses a fine avenue lined with lime trees, before reaching a small road. Turn left along this and cross the D313 (the Grande-Rue). On the right, on the D313, there is the marking – white and red crossed with an oblique white line – of an alternative route which must be taken when the Seine is in

flood. This alternative rejoins the GR2 in Courcelles-sur-Seine (see map).

Detour, *50 metres. Menhir called the* Gravier de Gargantua *(Gargantua's Gravel): walk along D313 towards Courcelles.*

The GR continues to the right along the towpath. Before you reach the barrage across the Seine, bear slightly to the right, and then left into the tarred Rue de La Roque.

5Km
1:15

Detour, *About 300 metres along this road, a narrow path between two fields leads to a small thicket at the bottom of a chalk cliff. Here you can see the tomb of Saint Ethbin, a 7th century Irish missionary. It is also possible to reach a strange cave hollowed out of the rockface half-way up the slope, which acted as a lookout post for centuries. At the top of the cliff (see map IGN ref 59) is a tower, known as Blanche of Castile's tower, which is the remains of a semaphore signal point.*

At La Roque the GR2 leaves the road, bending slightly left, to take a dirt track across enclosed fields. When approaching the outlying houses of Courcelles be careful not to take the good paved track on the right which leads to the D10; instead, keep below this road, staying on the grass track as far as the embankment of the D316 (formerly the N316).

D316
Detour, *1Km, 15 mins from the GR2 to Gaillon-Aubevoie station*

Detour, see left. Take the D316 to the left and cross the two bridges. After the railway bridge turn left down the steps to the station. From Gaillon station there is a 24 kilometre alternative route, marked in yellow, to the station at Saint-Pierre-du-Vauvray, along the left bank of the river.

GAILLON STATION
Ⓗ ✕ ▬ ▭

To reach the GR2, leave the station, go up the steps to the D316 and turn right along it. Cross the railway and then the Seine. Two hundred metres beyond the river, to the right and below the road, are the GR2 markings: straight ahead to Les Andelys or right to Vernon.

D316

Turn up to the right along the D316, and walk to Courcelles-sur-Seine.

COURCELLES-SUR-SEINE
♇ ▭ ▬
Junction with alternative flood route from Port-Mort.

Turn left into the Rue 13 Aout 1944, then left again into the path of Les Carrières. Take a broad paved track to Les Mousseaux. Follow the road as far as the cross, turn left there on to a dirt track overlooking a wide stretch of

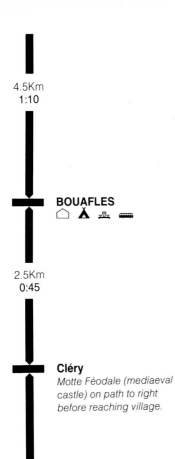

4.5Km
1:10

BOUAFLES

2.5Km
0:45

Cléry
*Motte Féodale (mediaeval
castle) on path to right
before reaching village.*

*Famous mediaeval castle
built within a single year
(1198–1199) by Richard the
Lionheart to protect Rouen.
View from top over Seine
valley.*

3.5Km
0:45

water (very limited waymarking), and then left along beside the Seine. Cross the canal by the footbridge, turn right towards another stretch of water, bear left to the western edge of the pine tree wood and follow the edge of the wood. Take a track heading north-east to a road. Follow this to the right. Turn left into the Rue des Mousseaux, then right into a lane between walls. Turn left into the street called the Chemin des Prés, then right into the lane of Les Quatre-Marmites to reach the D313 and the centre of Bouafles.

Follow the D313 to the left for 300 metres, past the Caravaning Base Nautique des Pilotins. Immediately after the church bear right up a lane and into the Colline wood. Narrow at first, the track broadens out into a wide forest avenue, which bends to the left at the top of the slope. Coming out of the wood, take a small tarred road, then leave it at the first bend and continue straight ahead on a dirt track (without waymarking) for 800 metres. On reaching another tarred road, the C21, turn right towards Cléry.

The GR crosses the village on a tarred road. After a bend to the right take the first track on the left, opposite the school. Although tarred at first, this becomes a dirt track following the edge of the wood for a kilometre. At the far end of this wood (see map IGN ref 147), continue in the same direction (north), as far as a road lined with trees, and turn left along it. Beyond the sports ground turn left on to a wide track through the wood, then bear right (north-west), on a footpath which first descends steeply and then levels out to reach the ruins of Château-Gaillard.

Take the GR past the ruins and their moat, leaving them on your left, then follow it down to the right, on one of several possible tracks, to the small, clearly visible asphalt road. Continue down this road to Le Petit-Andely; take the first street to the right, Rue Richard-Coeur-de-Lion, down to the D313. Turn left along this for 20 metres, then right into a short lane as far as the banks of the Seine. Take the promenade, Quai Grimaud, noting the beautiful lawns along the river; at the end, on a level with the Saint-Sauveur church, the promenade is closed to motor vehicles.

LES ANDELYS

12th century Gothic church of Saint Sauveur; some old houses; 13th–16th century church of Notre Dame; Saint-Clotilde fountain (a site of pilgrimage); ruins of Roman circus on Noyers hillside 2Km to north.

4.4Km
1:15

Val-Saint-Martin

2Km
0:30

Le Thuit

2Km
0:35

La Roquette
12th century chapel; fine viewpoint.

1Km
0:15

It is important to note that the next stretch of the GR2, as far as the locks at Poses, is more rugged, with marked changes of altitude. Paths across cliff faces should be used with care, especially when the ground is slippery.

Near the hospital turn right into the street which crosses the D313 and leads to Le Grand-Andely. About 100 metres from the crossroads, take a footpath which climbs straight up the hillside to the left as far as the reservoir. Circle around the reservoir to the left. Follow the clifftop in a generally north-west direction, as far as the Ermite (hermit) Rock, a vast cave-dwelling. Then bear northwards, following a footpath beside the Hogue wood. Descend steadily to a tarred path, and turn left along it to the hamlet of Val-Saint-Martin.

Take the D313 to the right, then the D126 towards Rouen. About 100 metres from the crossroads, take the footpath to the left through the wood. Cross the D126, walk through the wood again to reach the D126 once more. Follow this road to the right for 100 metres. Then take a dirt track off to the left, which brings you to the D126 yet again. Follow it once more to the left, walking beside the wall of the Château of Thuit, which has a fine gate, until you reach the small *mairie* in Le Thuit.

Turn left on to the path beside the château wall, past a pond. Turn left again on to a tarred track. Walk along it for 100 metres and then turn left on to a dirt track which leads to a small wood. Bear right as you go into the wood. On coming out of the wood, go right again on a footpath which zigzags down the hillside. As it reaches the bottom it roughly follows the contour line to the right beneath the cliffs. Then climb up another track to La Roquette.

Turn left on the track leading to the Mairie Square, then left again on to a wide path. Walk along this for the panoramic viewpoint at Notre-Dame-de-Bellegarde (112m). From here a very pretty path takes you down to the hamlet of La Roque.

LA ROQUE

Rock shaped like man's head.

At the bottom of the hill take the grassy path on the right, then the first track on the right coming in at an angle from the D313. Turn right along it for 200 metres, to the former gate-keeper's house at the level-crossing. The track leading on from here climbs up the hill to the south-west, and comes out on to a small tarred road. Turn left along it for 1.2 kilometres until you reach Blanche Farm. Turn right on to the paved track leading to the farm, then take the first dirt track on the left, for 1.5 kilometres. This brings you to another tarred road; turn right on to it and walk for 100 metres. Now turn left on to a footpath which runs through ·the wood. This takes you straight to the small village of Herqueville, where you turn right on to the D19 road. After 1.5 kilometres you come to Connelles.

8Km

2

Detour, *3.8Km, station at* **Saint-Pierre-du-Vauvray**

Route starts at second bend of D19.

CONNELLES

Deer park

Turn right after the church, then take the first footpath on the left, up on to the plateau. Take the second footpath on the right in the open field, and then turn left on to a tarred track with steep banks, heading towards Vatteville. After 2 kilometres you pass a pond and turn left on to a dirt track westwards through a small wood. On reaching the CAF climbing school, follow the route upwards across the rocks, heading north (see left). There is a fine view over the valley. Beyond the second group of rocks join a track which is suitable for vehicles, at a sharp bend. Immediately, turn left off it on to a small footpath which leads towards Vatteport, on the D19. After walking for 100 metres along the road, take a dirt track to the right leading to the hamlet of Senneville.

6Km

1:30

SENNEVILLE

Conservation site.

Without going as far as the hamlet itself, turn left on to the footpath which runs through a small group of houses. After 400 metres turn left on to a track through the wood, which leads to a panoramic viewpoint (113m). At the foot of this track turn left, then right, go through the gate (close it behind you), cross the field and climb the steep slope under the fence to meet the D20 road at a bend. Walk down the

2.5Km

0:40

road to the left for 350 metres then turn left on to a narrow footpath through bushes which brings you to another bend in the D20. Leave it again 50 metres lower down, turning left to reach the church at Amfreville-sous-les-Monts.

AMFREVILLE-SOUS-LES-MONTS

Take the D19 to the right for 50 metres until you reach the crossroads. Go up the D20 for 20 metres, then turn left on to the footpath which leads up the hillside. Half-way up follow a level curve round to the country footpath leading to Val-Pitan (see left). Cross the footpath. After another 150 metres, a footpath crosses the one you are on. Turn left on to it. This leads to the slope of Deux-Amants (Two Lovers) and the junction with the GR of the Pays de la Vallée de l'Andelle et du Pays de Bray, marked in yellow and red.

VAL-PITAN
at bottom of track.

Detour, *10 mins*
Château des Deux-Amants (Two Lovers)
panoramic view. Turn right.

SEINE LOCKS

Continue until you reach the D19. After walking along it for 100 metres to the right (north-west), turn left on to the track leading to the Seine locks (see left). At the western end of the locks take the tarred track – not the towpath – then the first track on the left, which crosses the Andelle. Immediately beyond the bridge, follow the river downstream and then walk along the Seine towpath to Le Manoir.

LE MANOIR

Turn right beyond the church, passing the *mairie*, and walk to the D321. Turn left along it for 200 metres, then right on to the country footpath leading to l'Essart Farm. Here turn left up to the Rouville wood. Turn left again (south) on to the dirt track in front of Le Solitaire farm, which you can see to your right. Cross the wood to Alizay.

5Km
1:30

ALIZAY

Take the first track to the right once you reach Alizay, and after a right angle bend, turn right again to reach the D321. Walk along it for 300 metres towards Igoville, then turn right (north)

73

on to the first track you see. This is tarred at first and then becomes a footpath. After walking across the plateau for 100 metres, cross a fence to the left, then a field and a gate. Opposite, a dirt track takes you back to the small tarred road between Igoville and Ymare. Turn left along it, taking a shortcut between bends in the road, and then head northwards, with the N15 (formerly the N13 *bis*) below to your right. Near a large lump of concrete climb the embankment, cross the road, and follow a track which runs northwards and then westwards beside La Sahatte wood.

Junction with the GR25
near Sotteville-sous-le-Val

After the junction with the GR25, the GR2 crosses the tarred road and take the dirt track directly opposite, which leads to the D91. Turn south-west along this for 100 metres, then take the dirt track to the right running between enclosed orchards. After 300 metres turn left on to a country footpath leading to a tarred track; turn right down this to Tourville-la-Rivière.

TOURVILLE-LA-RIVIÈRE
Ⱥ ᚏ

1.5Km
0:20

As you come into the village, turn right, then first left to the D7. Go left along it, across the carpark, and turn right by the railway fence. Go under the railway bridge and cross the Seine via the road bridge to Oissel.

OISSEL
🏠 Ⱥ ᚏ 🚂 🚋

9Km
2:30

After crossing the Seine, turn left and walk down to the river's edge. Follow the path along the river for 2.5 kilometres, then turn right, cross the D18 and, near a house, set off up the hill, heading westwards. Go up gently for 1 kilometre, passing first through coppiced trees, and then through taller trees. There is a fine view from the Pignon Rock. The wide path heads north, bends west for 400 metres, then forks to the south-west. Next, halfway down the slope, it switchbacks west before rejoining the wooded plateau. At an intersection take the first left turn; this takes you south-west along a beautiful forest avenue with a panoramic view. The path continues to the left, through copses to the Roche-Fouet viewpoint, where there are some castle ruins. Cross the clearing, still heading south-west, passing the remains of former cave-dwellings. Immediately after the last cave, turn right through the trees on to a narrow path which climbs up the bank. Along this path, which heads north-west and starts

75

descending later on, there are the ruins of a small Gallo-Roman temple, followed by traces of a Gallic fortified settlement. At the end of this forest avenue, take the second fork to the left which leads to the D132 by the car race-track of Les Essarts (*Nouveau Monde*) (New World), on the outskirts of Orival.

ORIVAL

Most of the village lies at the foot of the Seine cliffs. 15th–16th century church of Saint-Georges, partly hollowed out of rock, on Elbeuf road, past railway viaduct.

9.5Km
2:40

The GR2 does not go through Orival. At the junction of the D132 and the D64 (the La Bouille road), turn left along the path which runs below the D64. After 500 metres you enter a wood; 400 metres further on, the path descends, first north then north-west, to a crossroads. Turn left (south). After 700 metres, beyond a fork, turn right (west), on to the Chemin des Sangliers (the Boar Track) which goes up through the trees to the Lecomte Pool. Turn left along a tarmac path, which later becomes paved for 600 metres. Just before you reach the trees, turn right along a forest path. This brings you to another forest avenue, the Allée Saint Louis. At the crossing is the Belle-Arsène beech tree with its multiple trunks. Walk along the Allée Saint Louis to the left, until you come to a road, and then turn right. Walk under the railway and, shortly beyond, take the forest track, left, which climbs in a north–north-east direction. Turn left to pass under the motorway and head for the hamlet of La Maison Brulée.

LA MAISON BRULÉE

1870 war memorial

Turn left on the N180, towards Caen, for 50 metres, then right on to a footpath which leads to a small road. Turn left along the road for 50 metres until you reach the D132. Walk down this road and turn left on the 'ancienne côte de Bourgtheroulde' (the old Bourgtheroulde slope), with its fine view over the loop of the Seine, to La Bouille.

LA BOUILLE

A picturesque village with old houses. House of Hector Malot (novelist 1830–1907); ferry across the Seine. Junction for GR23.

6.2Km
1:30

Before reaching the ferry cross over the Seine to the right bank. Take the towpath heading downstream for 5.5 kilometres to the north-west. Crossing the river there is a panoramic view to the Caumont rocks on the left bank. Turn right on to the tarred road leading to the D67 at the Bellegarde Château on the northern edge of Saint-Pierre-de-Manneville.

SAINT-PIERRE-DE-MANNEVILLE

⌂ ▲ ✕ ⚓

Norman manors; 16th century church.

11.5Km
3

Without going into the village the GR2 turns left on the D67 and, opposite the entrance to the Bellegarde Château, turns right (east) on a dirt track towards the wood. At the edge of the wood cross the copse heading north-east, then left (north), following the contour line. This brings you to a track which you follow, still heading north, to a high tension cable. The track goes up to the right on the west side of the cable.

Turn left on the first track through the wood, then right on to a paved track for 700 metres (see left). Descend to the left through a hornbeam wood, to the bottom of the small valley. Follow the valley north-east to a plantation of pine trees on the plateau. Turn right as far as the first crossing, then turn south-east, and walk to a straight paved road which runs from Saint-Pierre to Dieppedalle. Turn left along this, past the Grand-Camp forest house, to the Petit-Charme forest house and, still going straight on, continue to the wildlife park. Turn left beside the enclosure containing boar and deer, and come out on a tarred road (Route de la Réunion). Turn left along it to the forest house of la Mare-des-Grès (Clay Pond). Turn right (north–north-east), on the Route Unique, leaving the forest house on the right.

Follow this beautiful forest avenue, which is straight but undulating, for 1.7 kilometres, to its junction with the Quevillon road across this and follow the footpath which runs parallel to the road, heading west. At the crossroads continue westwards, go through the hamlet of Genetey and continue to the wood. Turn right to go down through the wood and, on coming out, turn left (north-west), on to a dirt track to Saint-Martin-de-Boscherville.

SAINT-MARTIN-DE-BOSCHERVILLE

🏛 ⛺ ✕ 🚲 🚌

*Former abbey of
Saint-Georges, founded in
1050; 12th century church
(one of Normandy's most
notable Norman churches,
with very fine statues and
stained-glass windows).
Visits can be arranged in
advance by telephoning
35.76.36.54 or 35.76.36.55.*

9Km
2:10

SAINT-PIERRE-DE-VARENGEVILLE

⛺ 🚲

Bourg-Joly

4.3Km
1:40

From the church square continue northwards on the D67 for 400 metres. At the first fork bear left; at the second, bear left again for 400 metres. Then take the first track to the right, across the D982 (formerly the N182), up through the fields and across the D67. Walk along the track opposite, which runs parallel to the road into the forest. After walking through the wood for 600 metres, take a forest footpath to the left (north–north-west). After 800 metres this crosses the D67 and continues heading north-west, making a half-circle bend to the west to join a steep-sided tarred track down to the left for 500 metres. Turn right along a pretty track through the woods to the plateau near the Château of Perey. Turn left past the cemetery and, 400 metres further on, at the fork, bear left. After 1 kilometre this brings you to the Roman remains of Caesar's Camp. From here, walk down to the edge of the woods, enjoying the fine views, where you come to the D982 at the hamlet of La Fontaine. Turn right along the D982 for 200 metres. Close to an old chapel turn right on to the Sainte-Anne track into the woods. Go past the Gargantua farm and come out on the D43 at the hamlet of Bourg-Joly, on the western edge of Saint-Pierre-de-Varengeville.

The GR25 joins the path at Bourg-Joly.

From Bourg-Joly the GR2 will take you to Duclair. It follows the D43 left for 1 kilometre through a fine beech wood. Where the road forks, keep left on the tarmac road through the wood down to L'Anerie. On the right, close to the *Cercle de la Voile* (sailing club) carpark, take the path up to the west. At the top continue between enclosed fields until you rejoin the D43. Continue straight along it for 150 metres (west), then turn left on to a small path which slopes down to the south-west past some gardens. The path emerges on to an impressive avenue. At the end of this there is a path down to Duclair.

DUCLAIR

⌂ ⅄ ✗ ⚊ 🚋

A small town in an attractive setting. 12th–14th century church; tree-lined walk beside River Seine.

5Km
1:20

LE TRAIT

⌂

Naval shipyard; at Le Vieux-Trait, 16th century church with very fine statues inside.

8Km
2:15

From Duclair you take the D5, in the direction of Yvetot. Beyond the level crossing, cross the Austreberthe River and turn left into the street leading to the sports stadium. The GR2 begins here. Go up a steep slope and then along the edge of the woods until you reach the forestry house at La Haye d'Yainville. Follow the forest track for 400 metres to a junction (see map IGN ref 81). At this junction the GR23a branches off, opposite, towards Jumièges, while the GR2 continues to the right (west), towards the Mare aux Loups. Carry on in the same direction. After passing under some high-tension cables the path descends, crosses the D20 and, 800 metres further on, passes under a second line of cables. Walk along the edge of the wood for 200 metres, then turn right (north). For the next 500 metres you will be out of the woods, with extensive views over the Seine and the Brotonne forest. Immediately after you re-enter the woods, you will find a royal boundary marker on the left hidden in the undergrowth. Continue in the same direction until you reach the Le Trait water-tower.

The GR2 does not enter Le Trait. Continue along the route until you reach a reservoir. To the left of the reservoir, you will find a forest track. Follow this for 400 metres, then go steeply down to the left, along a fire-break. This leads into a shady track; turn right along it for 2.4 kilometres. The track runs along a ledge to the D63. Go up this road for 20 metres and turn left on to a level path with a fine view from La Mailleraye-sur-Seine to Villequier. Cross a sunken track and climb back up on to the ledge for 1 kilometre until it meets a forest track. Turn right along this, and go up to a tarmac forest road. Cross the road and bear north for 500 metres to the D64. Turn right along this road for 50 metres, then left (north), on to a small tarmac road. Follow this for 200 metres along the edge of the woods. Turn left on to a grass track in the wood and carry on for 1.3 kilometres. This brings you to a stony path bearing down to the left (west), to the *mairie* at Saint-Wandrille-Rançon.

SAINT-WANDRILLE-RANÇON

🏠 ⛺ ✕

Famous Benedictine abbey, founded 649 AD with 11th–16th century buildings (some parts open to public, but women not allowed in cloisters).

Detour, *400m*
Saint-Santurnin chapel
(10th century with 16th century façade): Continue along the road.

5.5Km
1:30

Here the GR211a branches off, right, towards Yvetot.

CAUDEBEC-EN-CAUX

🏠 ⛺ ✕ 🚉 🚌

15th century church of Notre Dame; group of 15th century houses on Place du Parvis; 13th century Maison des Templiers (Templars' House); view from Hôtel de Ville (Town Hall) terrace. Serious fire damage to the town in 1940.

From the abbey, turn left on to the D33 heading towards Rançon. Pass the 16th century 'Entombment'. When you reach the second bend in the road, continue to the right for 100 metres.

At this point there is a forest track opposite which winds northward through the Saint-Jacques forest for about 1.8 kilometres, then crosses a meadow to reach the D205. Turn left along the D205, and left again on to the D37. Walk along this as far as the 12th century Norman chapel at Rançon. Take a small tarred road opposite the chapel, heading west, then turn left on to a track which goes up through the wood. Turn left again on to a wide path. When the path bends sharply, take a track to the right, which leads to a path bordered with larches; turn left along it. Take the first path on the right which will bring you to the La Haye-des-Prés forest house, the junction point with the GR211a (see left).

Continue left (south–south-west), on the GR2, following a tarmac track, which comes up from Caudebec-en-Caux. After 150 metres turn left on to a beautiful grassy tree-lined avenue. At a bend, after about 700 metres, turn right on to a footpath, which passes a reservoir, and then emerges on to the Avenue de la Vignette, overlooking Caudebec and a loop of the Seine. Go left along the avenue for 50 metres, then turn right, down the steps to Caudebec-en-Caux.

Keep on the GR2, passing close to the *mairie*. Below the D982 go down some steps into a lane and continue along a track which leads westwards through clumps of trees.

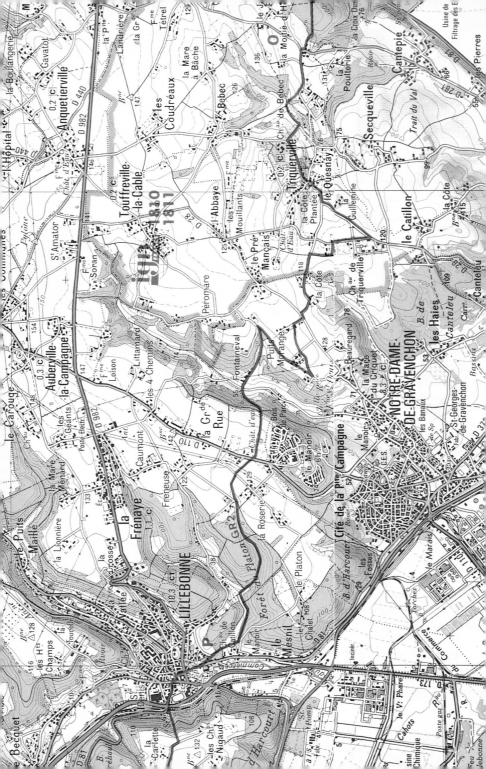

5Km
1:15

Junction with the GR211 at Le Calidu

At Le Calidu, the GR211 branches north (see left), while the GR2 joins the D982, only to leave it again immediately, heading towards the Barrey-va path, where the small chapel dedicated to sailors is a listed building. Turn right along the path, then right again on to the first path you come to which is leading upwards. After about 400 metres, turn left between two orchards. The path runs through the woods, turning into a paved track which passes in front of La Maison Blanche Château at La Guerche. At the second fork turn left, and left again on to a wide, straight path, which gradually becomes narrower as it approaches the church of Villequier. There is a fine view over the Seine.

VILLEQUIER

ⓗ Ӿ ✕ ⚓ 🚌

Victor Hugo museum.

5.5Km
1

Follow the GR2 straight down to the Seine, and turn right along the bank for 700 metres. Cross a tarmac road and take a grass track up through the woods (south-west), as far as a fire break. Turn right (north-west) along it until you reach a crossing. Bear left (south-west). At the next crossing (see map IGN ref 111), turn right (west) to leave the wood. Turn right again on to the road, then shortly afterwards turn left. After 600 metres turn right on to a track which leads down through the valley. Follow the valley path to the left until you reach a tarmac road. Turn right (west) along this road and continue as far as the château of Bébec. Turn left on to the paved path beside the château which takes you to Triquerville.

TRIQUERVILLE

Ӿ ⚓

10.5Km
2:40

Continue on the small tarmac road towards the south-west. When you are directly in front of the château de Triquerville, turn northwards and take the broad path to the left, then the grass track leading northwards. Turn left (west) on to a tarmac road which joins the D28. Turn left along it, then right, then left on to a footpath heading west between fences. Next, take the dirt track to the right, which leads to a tarmac road. Turn left along it and continue down to the Fontaineval Valley. Climb back up to the plateau, passing a copse and crossing a field towards a water-tower, before reaching the D110. Turn right, then immediately left on to a dirt track through arable land. Cross two meadows and enter the Platon forest in the valley. When the path emerges

into a clearing, turn left (south-west) on to the path which leads to Lillebonne.

LILLEBONNE

Substantial Roman ruins; archaeological museum.

9Km
2:30

Leave the town on the west side, and rejoin the GR2 at the level crossing on the D81. The route goes up through the woods to the south for about 50 metres, then west on to the open plateau, where it continues along a small tarmac road. Take the first paved path to the left (south), then turn right on to a track, which passes through the Harcourt wood and then crosses a plain, from where there is a fine view over the Seine valley. Cross a tarmac road, then go through a farmyard on the public right of way, taking care to close the gates. The path continues along the bottom of a small valley, heading mainly in a south-westerly direction. It passes in front of Bellevue Farm and joins the tarmac road to Le Bout-de-Ville. Take the D17 southward, and after 150 metres turn left on to a small tarmac road which goes through a hamlet, across a field and through a wood near a radar station. After a sharp bend, the path heads north, then west, descending steeply to the D17, which takes you into Tancarville.

TANCARVILLE

12th–14th century castle; suspension bridge.
At the Tancarville bridge the GR23 joins the GR2.

5.5Km
1:20

Pick up the GR2 which leaves Tancarville via the D39 to the south-west. At the first bend leave the road and, continuing in the same direction, take the path up through the wood called Courte Cote. Cross the D39 a bit further on, then turn left on to a footpath. Turn left again (south-west) at the second junction. Cross the D39 again, then the D910. Just below it turn right on to the small path which curves westward between trees and fields. Where it joins the tarmac road, turn left, and after 500 metres turn right on to a dirt track to La Cerlangue.

LA CERLANGUE

Church with stone bell tower. 11th century Norman church with crypt and frescoes.

4Km
1

From here, go right until you reach the D39. Opposite the church turn left, then left again, then right on to a dirt track heading south-west. This leads to a tarred road; turn right and then immediately left on to a paved path. The paving becomes tarmac as the path passes through the small village of Saint-Jean-d'Abbetot (see left). Beyond the church turn left, left again, and then right on to a path to the south-west, leading to Saint-Vigor-d'Ymonville.

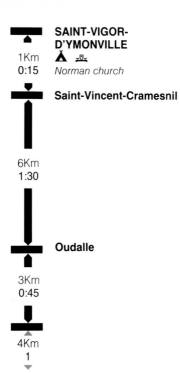

SAINT-VIGOR-D'YMONVILLE

1Km
0:15

Norman church

As you approach this market town take a path to the right (north-west), which becomes a dirt track. Cross the D112 and continue in the same direction to Saint-Vincent-Cramesnil.

Saint-Vincent-Cramesnil

6Km
1:30

As you reach the village, turn left and then immediately right on to a tarmac path heading north-west. Cross the D80, walk between two arable fields and turn left (south-west), on to a dirt track which takes you into the cluster of houses called Le Catillon, then bears right to a wooded valley. Go left (south-west) along the valley to the hamlet of Les Fontaines. From there take the tarmac road, leaving it for a footpath to the right which heads up through the trees to Oudalle.

Oudalle

3Km
0:45

Where the footpath rejoins the tarmac road turn right, then left at the crossroads. Next take the small tarmac road to the right, which is lined with beech trees and leads to a wooded valley.

4Km
1

Alternative route From Oudalle to Gournay. Turn right and walk along the wooded valley just mentioned until you reach Saint-Aubin-Routot.

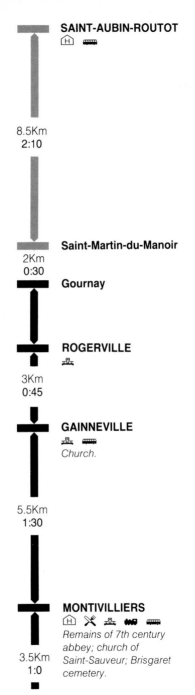

SAINT-AUBIN-ROUTOT

8.5Km
2:10

Saint-Martin-du-Manoir

2Km
0:30

Gournay

ROGERVILLE

3Km
0:45

GAINNEVILLE
Church.

5.5Km
1:30

MONTIVILLIERS
Remains of 7th century
abbey; church of
Saint-Sauveur; Brisgaret
cemetery.

3.5Km
1:0

From here, take the street heading north, cross the N13 *bis*, and at the hamlet of Carouge, take the second turning on the right. Cross the D34 and continue to Épretot. At the church, turn left on to a small tarmac road, then take the first left again. At the D34 go left, and after 100 metres turn right on to a small track which takes you through the hamlet of Bois-Gaillot. About 500 metres after leaving the hamlet, turn right on to a dirt track, which goes round La Vignotière and then swings north-west. Cross the D34, then follow the edge of the wood to the left (northwards). The path curves to the right across some fields and then passes through the market town of Saint-Martin-du-Manoir.

From the village, go south and then west to reach the hamlet of Gournay.

Go left along the valley to the D982. Turn right, walk along it until you reach the D111. Cross it and take the path through the woods up to Rogerville.

Leave the village at the western exit, heading towards Gainneville. Take the path on the left leading down to the valley. Climb up again, heading right until you reach the outskirts of Gainneville.

Do not enter the town, but instead turn left on to the small road which leads to the N13 *bis*. Turn left on to the road and walk along it to the crossroads. Turn right. At the entrance to Pradon Farm, cross the meadow, following the line of trees towards the north-west. When you reach the road at a point where there is a sharp bend, keep to the path, bearing left until you reach another road. Turn right along the road. Where it meets the D34, turn left and walk along it to the little village of Gournay. Here you will find a path heading north-west to Montivilliers.

The walk starts at the Montivilliers fairground, where the GR2 branches off from the GR21 to Fécamp. To pick up the waymarking, find the Rue Oscar-Germain, then the Rue Victor-Lesuer; the first sign is on a telegraph pole in front of the abbey. When you come to the road (D32), go up the path leading off through the

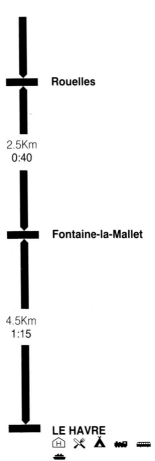

Rouelles

2.5Km
0:40

Fontaine-la-Mallet

4.5Km
1:15

LE HAVRE

*The city was almost
completely destroyed in the
Second World War and
subsequently rebuilt. This is
primarily a major commercial
and industrial port. Cultural
centre designed by Oscar
Niemeyer.*

trees opposite you, then cross the open
ground heading south-east. Shortly after the
Ardennes farm, walk back down to rejoin the
D32.

Follow the D32 through the outskirts of
Rouelles, passing the sports stadium, until you
reach a stone-built farmhouse. Turn right and
then, 20 metres further on, between the farm
and a field, turn left on to the track which runs
along the river; the poor condition of the river-
bank may make this an awkward stretch so
follow the markings with care. When you get to
the hamlet of Le Moulin turn right beside a
concrete wall. From there, the path runs clearly
to Fontaine-la-Mallet.

In the main street, which is lined with plane
trees, take the right turn which leads to the
cemetery. Continue as far as the water-tower
and turn left along a dirt track. The path then
turns left again, taking you through a wood,
across a road (D52) and into the Montgeon
forest. When you have crossed the forest, you
can either leave it close to the Place Jenner
(from where you can reach the centre of town
via the Jenner tunnel, the Cours de la
République and the railway station, a walk of
30 minutes) or continue to the La Frileuse gate.
A number 12 bus from the Rue Louis-Blanc, on
the right, will take you to the railway station.

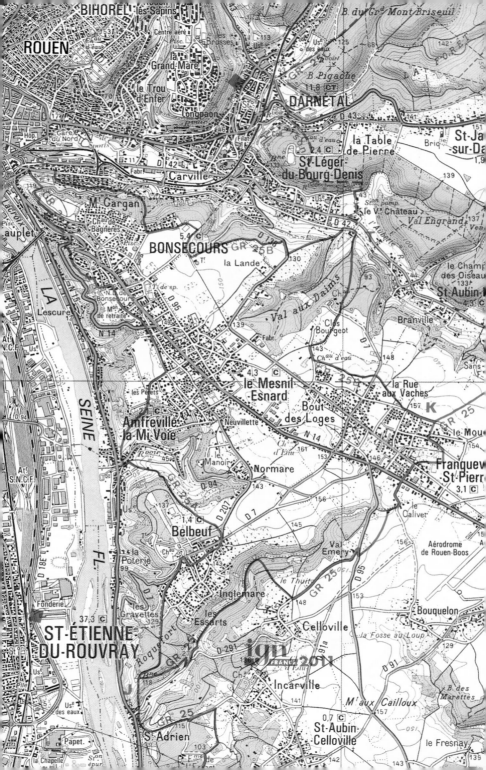

WALK 4

ROUEN

🏛️ ⛪ 🍴 🚉 🚌 🚃 ℹ️

Cathedral; several churches with fine carvings; Palais de Justice (Law Courts); Tour Jeanne-d'Arc (Joan of Arc's Tower); many pedestrianised streets which make it possible to enjoy looking at the 15th–16th century façades; the Gros Horloge (Great Clock).

5.5Km
1:15

The waymarking for the GR25a starts in Rue Annie-de-Pène, at the west corner of the Mont-Gargan cemetery, and goes up to a road junction where it turns right; after 200 metres it turns down, right, by the Noyers (walnut tree) path to the Bonsecours urban area.

Cross the road, go down the steps, go up the street and turn right into the Rue de la Paix, then left onto the Berthet steps. Turn right, then after 200 metres left onto a former tramway track leading to the Bon-Secours church; from here there is a panoramic view over south Rouen. Take the Rue G.-Loquet on the left of the church, then Rue Le-Bourgeois, right; this crosses the N14 road and becomes the paved way to allotments. Turn right towards Les Perets then take the path down to Amfreville-la-Mi-Voie.

AMFREVILLE-LA-MI-VOIE

🍷 🚉 🚌

2Km
0:30

Take the road to the cemetery, then turn left on to a dirt path which meets the D7 at Belbeuf.

BELBEUF

🍷 🚉

Château; dovecote; chapel.

3Km
0:45

From the D7 take the first turning on the right; follow this street to the third crossroads where you turn right to rejoin the D7 at a point facing the château. Turn left along the D7, then take the left fork on to a road, which turns into a dirt track running through the Roquefort wood. As you come out of the wood (see map IGN ref 118), you will find a GR sign indicating the junction with the GR25.

Junction with GR25a

5Km
0:10

From the junction, you now follow the GR25, the path down towards the road (D291) and the small hamlet of Saint-Adrien.

SAINT-ADRIEN

🏛️ 🍴 🚌

3Km
0:45

The walk leaves the D291 on the southern side of Saint-Adrien, climbing up to the left along a steep-sided path which then joins a road. Take the first path to the right, which loops back round to meet the road again (map ref 103).
Go straight down (south) until you come to a sharp bend to the left; there the path goes down to the right into a wooded valley, becoming a dirt track. After about 200 metres walking along the valley, the track becomes a

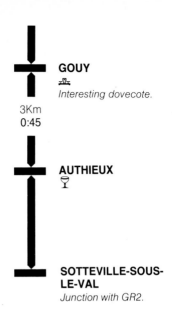

GOUY

Interesting dovecote.

3Km
0:45

AUTHIEUX

**SOTTEVILLE-SOUS-
LE-VAL**

Junction with GR2.

road which takes you into the outskirts of Gouy.

In Gouy turn almost immediately right on to a sunken path leading down through the wood to the Côte Jore. Continue, crossing the main road (N15), to Port-Saint-Ouen: there, the footpath climbs up steps and on up through the wood to the Clos du Mouchel. It will take you directly to Authieux.

The path cuts straight through Authieux, crossing the road (D13), and becomes a dirt track running south to Sahatte wood. Here, on the western edge of the wood, the GR25 meets the GR2 (see map ref 1), turn right onto the GR2, near the village of Sotteville-sous-le-Val.

WALK 5

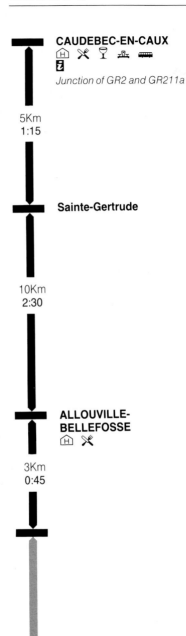

5Km
1:15

10Km
2:30

3Km
0:45

CAUDEBEC-EN-CAUX

Junction of GR2 and GR211a

The GR211 begins at 'Le Calidu', on the GR2 at the western edge of Caudebec. Go down the small path to the right, then immediately turn left on to the path which crosses the D982. Continue through the wood and, after 500 metres, take a path to the right which crosses a paved track to reach a forest track. Turn right and follow it through the wood along the Sainte-Gertrude valley. After 3 kilometres, turn right on to a path emerging from the forest, and cross the small bridge into Sainte-Gertrude.

Sainte-Gertrude

Beyond the church, turn west on to the D40. After 150 metres take the path going up to the right (north), and continue along it for 2 kilometres. This takes you past L'Ouraille. Continue following the path westwards to Le Cul de Sac, then take the footpath down to the left. This joins a road: turn right along it. Where the road bends sharply left (see map IGN ref 57), bear right towards Le Désert. One kilometre further on, fork right (north-east) up the valley, which brings you to the D104. Turn left along the road to La Fèvrerie; turn right and go through Le Hamelet (see left). At the first crossroads turn right, then left at the next crossroads, and head for Allouville-Bellefosse.

ALLOUVILLE-BELLEFOSSE

Take the D34 north-east towards Yport. When you come to the edge of the village, take the first dirt track to the left as far as the D110, and cross it. Follow the path north-west, passing La Galandière. Continue straight on to the edge of Valliquerville and then take the second turn to the right. This leads first to the centre, and then the château of Valliquerville.

Alternative route (GR11a) from Caudebec-en-Caux to Valliquerville. The route begins outside the forest house at La Haye-des-Prés on the GR2, about 1 kilometre to the north-east of Caudebec. Pass the forest house (coming from the direction of Caudebec) and take the second grass path to the right (north). This leads to the road at La-Haye-des-Prés: turn right along it, and then take the first road to the left, towards l'Enfer. At the crossroads, turn

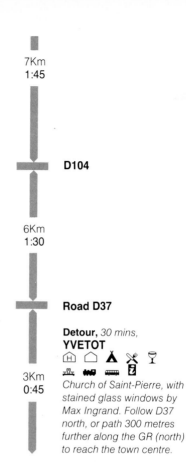

7Km
1:45

D104

6Km
1:30

Road D37

Detour, *30 mins,*
YVETOT

3Km
0:45

Church of Saint-Pierre, with
stained glass windows by
Max Ingrand. Follow D37
north, or path 300 metres
further along the GR (north)
to reach the town centre.

right (north-east) along the road which crosses the D490 at La Lance. Walk down through the wood and across the D33 to reach the D89 and turn along it to the left. At the crossroads, fork left towards Touffreville. At the next junction bear right and go up the valley through Caux wood. At the far end of the wood turn right (south-east), and when you reach Befolet bear left (north-east) to join the D104.

Follow the D104 to the left and, after 300 metres, turn right (north-east) along a dirt track. The way through the wood is not easy; go across the field or through the wood, and down to the D5. Turn left, and beyond the inn at Le Val-au-Cesne, turn left on a grass footpath going north-west to reach the hamlet of Le Maroc. Continue up the valley to the left (north-west) to a filter-station; there you cross the D37.

After crossing the D37, continue along a path which runs parallel to the road. After 300 metres, bear left and walk up the footpath through the valley, and round the southern side of the Château of Auzebosc. Cross the D131 to reach the church at Auzebosc.

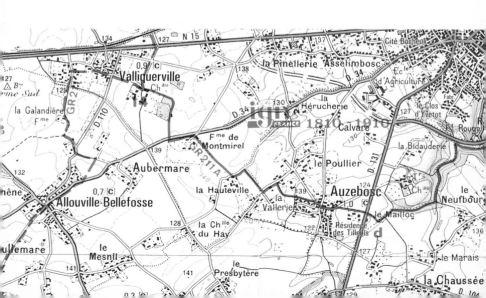

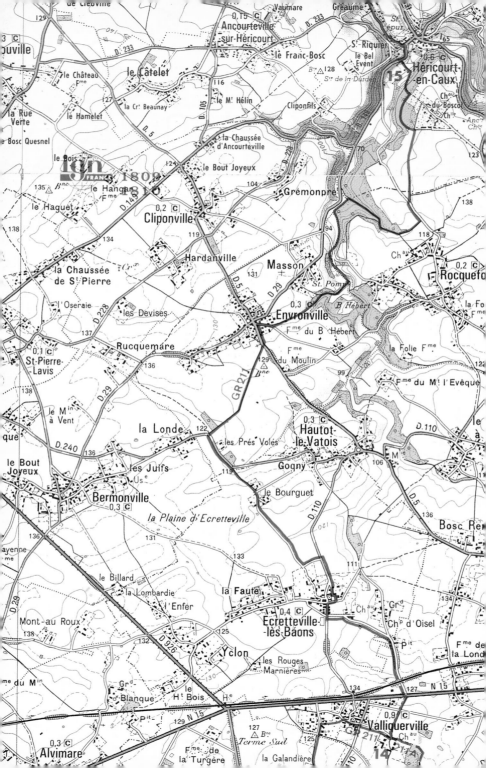

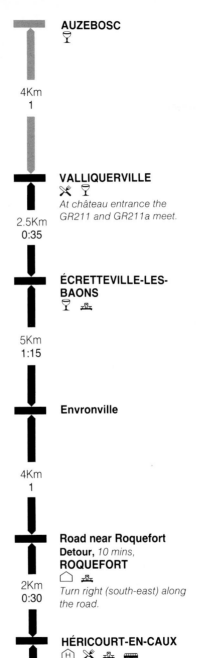

AUZEBOSC

4Km
1

VALLIQUERVILLE
At château entrance the GR211 and GR211a meet.

2.5Km
0:35

ÉCRETTEVILLE-LES-BAONS

5Km
1:15

Envronville

4Km
1

Road near Roquefort
Detour, *10 mins,*
ROQUEFORT
Turn right (south-east) along the road.

2Km
0:30

HÉRICOURT-EN-CAUX

From Auzebosc church follow the route to the north-west along the road. Turn left (west) on to a grass path, which leads to another road (going to the hamlet of Le Pouillier on the right). Turn left along this road, then take the first path to the right, and walk to La Hauteville. From the hamlet, turn right (north-west), which brings you to Montmirel Farm. At the crossroads take the D34 left, then the footpath to the right (north) which takes you to the château at Valliquerville.

The GR211 continues northwards to the left along a paved path which crosses the N15 and continues along a road. At the fork at Le Petit Champ d'Oisel, keep left. Walk beside the castle (ruins on the farm). At the crossroads, turn right (north), to reach the centre of Écretteville-les-Baons.

Follow the D110 (north), bear left after 750 metres, then right on to the road which goes past Le Bourguet and joins a path which carries straight on to the D240. Continue onwards in the same direction, passing Les Près Volés. Where the road bends left (see map IGN ref 122) turn right on to a path heading north-east. This joins the D5; turn left along it to reach Envronville.

Here, the GR211 bears back to the right at the first crossroads. Walk along the road for 250 metres and then turn left (north-east) down through the Hèbert wood. Next, join a track on the left, and when it reaches the road, go straight across, through the gate, and along the path beside the wood. This brings you to a wooded valley which you follow until you meet the road near Roquefort.

Turn left along this road and take the first dirt track to the right, through the fields. On the edge of the wood take the path to the left. At the bottom of the avenue leading from the Château du Boscol, bear left. Continue down to the D149 and into the village of Héricourt-en-Caux.

Keep to the GR21 as it passes in front of the Héricourt Sports Ground. At the crossroads take the D233 to the left, then the first turning to the right and walk along the River Durdent.

11Km
2:45

8Km
2

GRAINVILLE-LA-TEINTURIÈRE
🏠 ✖ ☍ ⎈

Departure point for the GR211b towards Fécamp.

Cross the D106 and take the public road to the watercress beds. Join the D105, cross the bridge, and head northwards towards the church at Auffay. After some zig-zag bends, turn left. When you reach a crossroads which is on flat ground, turn left and walk along the path in front of the château. Continue for 2 kilometres, then take the path to the left, which leads down through the woods. Cross the D131, then take the D150 to cross the Durdent at Le Hanouard. Now, take the first path on the right, cross a field, and climb up to the left. The route now takes you north-west through several fields to the lower edge of the wood, and brings you, after a further 2 kilometres, to the church at Grainville-la-Teinturière.

Pass the *salle des fêtes* (public hall), then follow a footpath to the left, heading north-west through the Roquette wood. It comes out of the wood at La Roquette, on a road which should be followed as far as the second crossroads. Turn left there (north-west) towards Barville. Pass the church and cross the River Durdent in front of the Château de Cany. Carry on to the level crossing (northwards), then walk along the D̓31 for 250 metres and bear left on a path leading to La Ruelle. At the crossing, turn right (north) to reach Les Criquets and then the church of Cany-Barville.

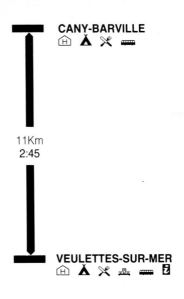

CANY-BARVILLE

11Km
2:45

VEULETTES-SUR-MER

At Cany the GR heads north along the D268, then up the first road to the right, leading to Clasville. On reaching the crossroads there, take the road right (north), then turn left on to the first dirt track, which takes you to the D271. Turn right and walk along this road to Le Bout-Enragé. Now turn right on to the D69; as it slopes down, and after a bend, turn left on to a path (north) which continues steeply down into the wooded Bascourt Valley, and leads to the hamlet of Saint-Gilles. Here, take the D268 to the left and, at the second crossroads, cross the D68. On the right is the junction with the GR21 which heads towards Saint-Valéry. The GR211 and GR21 now continue to follow a footpath heading north-west along the River Durdent to Veulettes-sur-Mer.

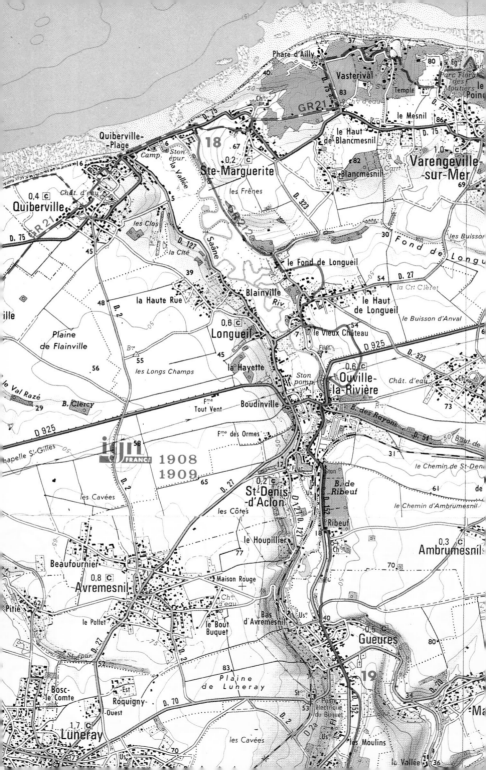

WALK 6

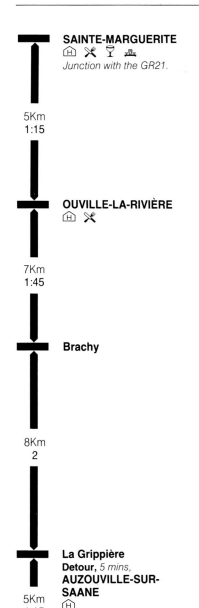

SAINTE-MARGUERITE

⌂ ✕ ⏐ ⚓
Junction with the GR21.

5Km
1:15

OUVILLE-LA-RIVIÈRE

⌂ ✕

7Km
1:45

Brachy

8Km
2

La Grippière
Detour, *5 mins,*
AUZOUVILLE-SUR-
SAANE
⌂

5Km
1:15

From La Grippière turn right (south-west) and cross the River Saane.

The GR212 begins on the D75, 1 kilometre to the west of the centre of Sainte-Marguerite, and follows the right bank of the River Saâne. At Le Fond de Longueil, take the D323, right, then turn left on to a dirt track. This loops round, crosses the D323 and leads to a church. About 100 metres beyond the church, turn left on to a path which first leads eastwards and then south. Cross the D925. After a short while, you come back to the D925. This time, turn left along it (south) heading to the centre of Ouville-la-Rivière.

At the crossroads in the centre of the village, take the D152, left, for 2 kilometres. On the edge of the Ribeuf Wood, fork left and pass in front of a chapel. A dirt track leads to the D152 at Gueures. As you leave the village, turn left along a dirt track. After a little way, you will skirt a small wood and then cross ploughed fields. When the track crosses a road, turn right and rejoin the D108. Turn right and follow it to the church at Brachy.

Still keeping to the eastern slope of the Saâne valley, leave the mill road by turning left (south) on to a footpath, which passes through the Saint-Ouen wood and joins a road leading first south and then south-west, to Bas-de-Royville. The GR does not go into Rainfreville but continues on a footpath to the Églemesnil dairy. Turn left here, on to the D107, then at the first crossroads, turn right on to the D507e. After 100 metres, fork right. After a while, you will come out on the D149. Continue along it to the crossroads. Leaving Saâne-Saint-Just to your right, take the road opposite (south). The GR passes through Le Carel and reaches the D55 at La Grippière.

From La Grippière, the GR follows the D55 for 300 metres and then continues along the river-bank, passing through Beau-Soleil, La Filature, and Mont-Varin until it reaches the D23. Go south along it into Val-de-Saâne-Anglesqueville.

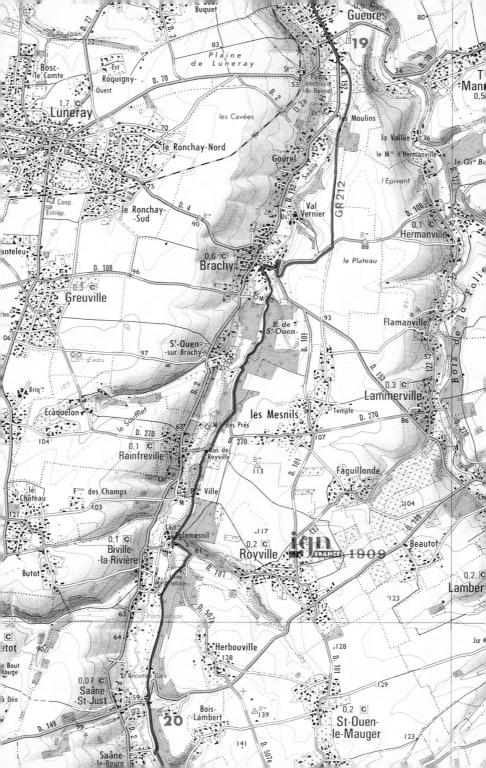

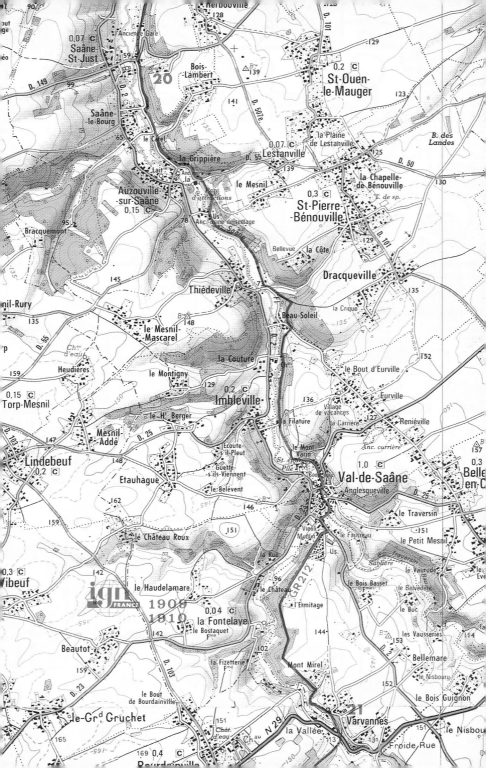

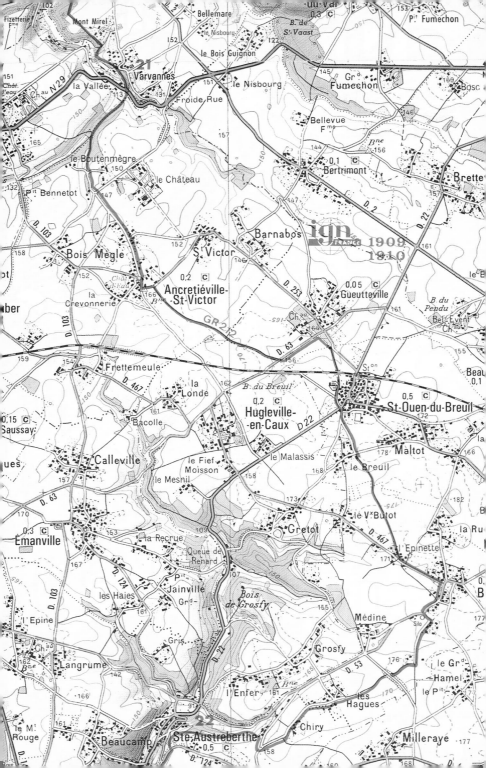

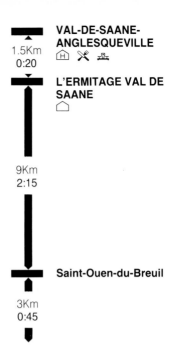

1.5Km
0:20

VAL-DE-SAANE-ANGLESQUEVILLE

As you leave this market town on the D2, heading south, take a path to the right, leading to L'Ermitage.

L'ERMITAGE VAL DE SAANE

9Km
2:15

From the Érmitage rest-hut, continue southwards through Mont-Mirel, where there is a fine beech hedge, and the source of the River Saâne. Cross the N49 and follow a wooded valley, which takes you south-west, then south. This comes out on to a road at Boutenmègre. Leaving the château with its handsome dovecote on your left, follow the road as far as Ancretiéville-Saint-Victor. From there take a dirt track south-east to the D63, and turn left along it. Just before Gueutteville turn right on to a grass track, which passes under the railway and reaches the outskirts of Saint-Ouen-du-Breuil.

Saint-Ouen-du-Breuil

3Km
0:45

From Saint-Ouen-du-Breuil, continue southwards, crossing the D22 and taking the road south. After 100 metres take a grass track along the bank of the River Breuil. When you reach the D467, at l'Épinette, turn left along it, heading south-east to Butot.

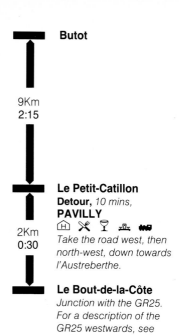

Butot

9Km
2:15

Le Petit-Catillon
Detour, *10 mins,*
PAVILLY

2Km
0:30

*Take the road west, then
north-west, down towards
l'Austreberthe.*

Le Bout-de-la-Côte
*Junction with the GR25.
For a description of the
GR25 westwards, see
p. 21.*

Leave Butot on the D53 (south-west). At the grain silo, turn left and after the second farm bear right (south-west), towards Les Hagues and Chiry. At the forked junction (see map IGN ref 158) take the right turn north for 150 metres, then bear left (west) on the footpath leading to the D124 at Sainte-Austreberthe. Take this road, heading south-west, along the wood's edge. Cross the D6 at Rougemont and take the D44. At La Tuilerie, turn right, heading due south, to Le Petit-Catillon.

From Le Petit-Catillon, continue left (east) along the path to La Caillotère. Five hundred metres further to the south-east, at Le Bout-de-la-Côte, is the junction with the GR25.

WALK 7

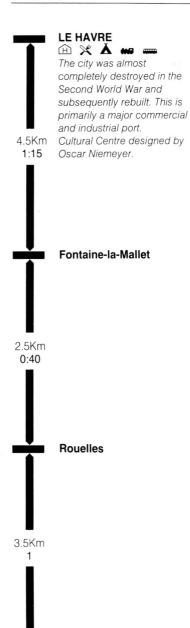

LE HAVRE

The city was almost completely destroyed in the Second World War and subsequently rebuilt. This is primarily a major commercial and industrial port. Cultural Centre designed by Oscar Niemeyer.

4.5Km
1:15

Fontaine-la-Mallet

2.5Km
0:40

Rouelles

3.5Km
1

The walk starts on the edge of the Montpeon forest. The path, the GR2, can be picked up at either of two points of entry to the forest: the La Frileuse gate, near Rue Louis-Blanc, which can be reached by bus from the railway station, or a gate near Place Jenner, which is half an hour's walk from the station via the Jenner tunnel and the Cours de la République. Follow the track through the forest, then across a road (D52) and through another wood; the path will then turn to the right along a dirt track. When you reach the water-tower on the outskirts of Fontaine-la-Mallet, turn right again, this time on to a road. It will lead you past the cemetery and bring you out in the main street, lined with plane trees.

From the main street, the GR2 runs down a turning to the left. At the first crossroads take the second right, which runs out into open countryside towards the little hamlet of Le Moulin. There, at a concrete wall, the path turns left and runs along the river: the poor condition of the river-bank may make this an awkward stretch, so follow the markings with care. As you come towards Rouelles, you will see a stone-built farmhouse: the path turns right there, between the farm and a field, and then, after another 20 metres, reaches the main road (D32). Turn left on to the road and walk along and past the sports stadium.

Follow the road round through the outskirts of Rouelles. The path leaves it again soon, turning left up a slope. You pass the Ardennes farm and then head north-west across open ground until you come to a wooded area and meet the D32 again. Cross over and walk up the road opposite, which takes you past the abbey, up the Rue Victor-Lesueur and then the Rue Oscar-Germain to the centre of Montivilliers.

MONTIVILLIERS

Remains of 7th century abbey; church of Saint-Sauveur; Brisgaret cemetery.

Find your way to the Montivilliers fair-ground, where the GR2 meets the GR21 to Fécamp. From there the path runs along Rue Louis-Lequette; after 400 metres turn left on to the lane to La Clinarderie, and cross the D111. When you reach Mélay farm veer left, then take the first path on the right; the track, going across the meadow, is not very easy to see. Cross a tarmac road and continue along a path which joins another; as this twists to the left, it meets the footpath which takes you down to Rolleville.

ROLLEVILLE

16th century manor-house and dovecote.

3Km
0:50

The GR does not go into Rolleville; it crosses the main road (D32), then runs along a small road to the left leading to Notre-Dame-du-Bec, where there is a *château*; 250 metres beyond the church turn right on to a footpath. This leads to Turretot.

TURRETOT

Beyond the church take the road on the right. Where the road bends to the right, the GR goes off to the left, crossing the D125, towards the edge of Les Châtaigniers farm, where it turns left. At the first fork keep right — you will go past a Protestant church — and on reaching the D79 turn left, then left again beyond the railway track. You will cross the D125a, then three small tarmac roads. After passing a cluster of houses called Les Brouettes, fork right along the grass path, which will take you to Gonneville-la-Mallet.

8Km
2

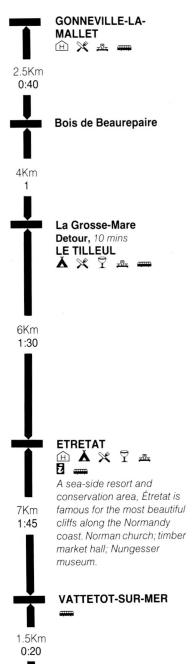

GONNEVILLE-LA-MALLET

2.5Km
0:40

Bois de Beaurepaire

4Km
1

La Grosse-Mare
Detour, *10 mins*
LE TILLEUL

6Km
1:30

ETRETAT

A sea-side resort and conservation area, Étretat is famous for the most beautiful cliffs along the Normandy coast. Norman church; timber market hall; Nungesser museum.

7Km
1:45

VATTETOT-SUR-MER

1.5Km
0:20

At the edge of this market town take the D74 right (north-east) to La Mare Binet; then take the path left (north) to La Ferme Baril and, beyond that, the beginning of the Beaurepaire valley. Continue northwards until you reach the junction with the GR21b on the edge of the Bois de Beaurepaire.

The GR21b goes off to the right towards Yport (see p.129). Keep to the GR21, continuing northwards up the valley to the end of the wood; then follow the road for 600 metres. Beyond the hamlet of La Chaumières turn left, walking west then north-west, to reach La Grosse-Mare.

The GR21 runs north across the three roads running out of La Grosse-Mare, then turns left to cross the D940. After 250 metres on a side road, turn off to the right towards a water-tower; shortly after passing it, as you approach Valaine, take the first turn to the left. Go down into the wood and turn right along the short Antifer valley. At the top of the way down to the beach, the GR turns right along the coast.

This coastal path may be dangerous in wet or foggy weather. Keep well away from the edge, even in fine conditions. Before the descent into the resort of Étretat, there is a fine view of the coast from a recess in the cliff. Continue along beside the golf course to reach Étretat.

The GR goes behind the Roches-Blanches Hotel to the flat open ground and continues along the cliff-top: keep away from the edge even in fine weather. It crosses the small Curé valley, typical of the Pays de Caux region, then the Vattetot and Étigue valleys. Turn right along the road, then take the first footpath on the left back up to the flat higher ground, and follow it through to the outlying houses of Vattetot-sur-Mer.

The GR leaves Vattetot with the village away to the right and continues along a path down through a wood to meet the D211 just before Vaucottes. Turn left and follow the road into the village.

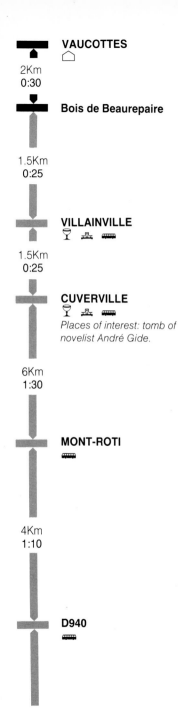

VAUCOTTES

2Km
0:30

Bois de Beaurepaire

1.5Km
0:25

VILLAINVILLE

1.5Km
0:25

CUVERVILLE

Places of interest: tomb of novelist André Gide.

6Km
1:30

MONT-ROTI

4Km
1:10

D940

From Vaucottes the GR follows the D211 back up on to the cliff-top. After a big hairpin bend take the first path to the left, from which there are excellent views and follow it to Yport.

Alternative route from Bois de Beaurepaire to Yport (GR21b). The GR21b leaves the GR21 in the valley of Beaurepaire wood. While the GR21 heads north towards La Grosse-Mare, the GR21b turns right, leaving the valley, and leads to the hamlet of Le Centre. From here you take the second turn to the left, northwards to Villainville.

At Villainville, the GR21b crosses the D39 and turns left. Heading due north, keep going straight on, crossing the D74 and the D239. Now, take the road which leads up to the centre of Cuverville.

At the crossroads in front of Cuverville church, turn left and take the road down to the road junction, where you turn left again. After the hamlet of Le Fond-des-Bois, as the road swings left, the GR21b turns right (east) into the Bois des Loges. It travels the entire length of the wood, following the valley as far as the D72 road. Turn right along the D72 until you reach the coach stop in the village of Mont-Roti.

After passing the coach stop, turn left off the D72. At the top of the slope, bear left again, then right a little further on. Follow the road as far as the D74. Turn right (east) along the D74. Pass a transformer, then turn right, leaving the road, and carry straight on, between two farms, to Le Coquet. Turn left here and, where the D74 crosses the D11, take a small paved footpath leading to the right. After a while it becomes a grass track, and then joins a road. Turn left at this point, to rejoin the D11. Turn right along the D11 and cross the railway. This brings you to the D940 road.

Cross the D940 and continue along the D11; 250 metres further on, beside a transformer, the road forks right on to a grass footpath which leads down to a wood. Continue up again to Les Hogues. Take the road left (north) past the IGN marker (see map IGN ref 97). At the entrance to the Forty Acre Wood is the

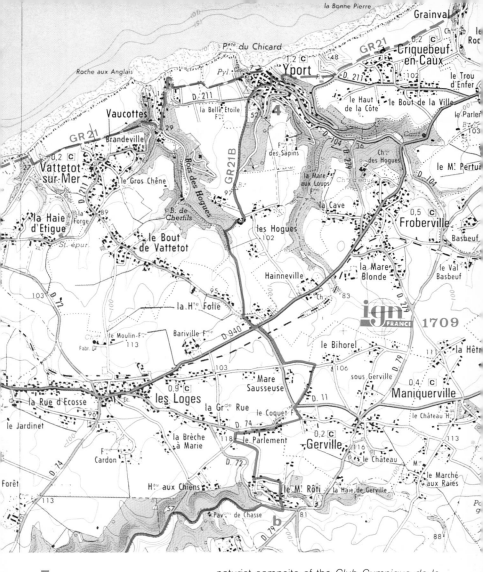

4.5Km
1:10

naturist campsite of the *Club Gymnique de la Porte Océane*, for which an FFN (Federation of French Naturists) permit is required. Turn left off the road on to a footpath, which runs along the edge of the wood. Cross the D211 and continue along the road, going down. Take the first street on the right. The GR enters the town via the Rue de la Gardine and the Rue de Jean-Feuilloley and leads you to the centre of Yport.

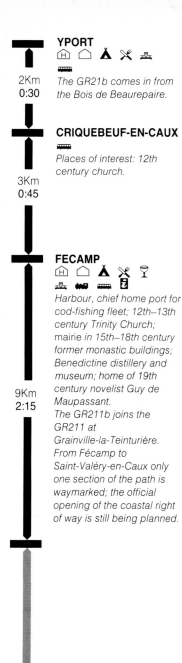

YPORT

2Km
0:30

The GR21b comes in from the Bois de Beaurepaire.

CRIQUEBEUF-EN-CAUX

Places of interest: 12th century church.

3Km
0:45

FECAMP

Harbour, chief home port for cod-fishing fleet; 12th–13th century Trinity Church; mairie in 15th–18th century former monastic buildings; Benedictine distillery and museum; home of 19th century novelist Guy de Maupassant.
The GR211b joins the GR211 at Grainville-la-Teinturière.
From Fécamp to Saint-Valéry-en-Caux only one section of the path is waymarked; the official opening of the coastal right of way is still being planned.

9Km
2:15

Follow the GR along the street opposite the jetty, and on the far side of the square turn left on to a small path up to the plateau in a series of hairpin bends. At the wayside cross turn left, then continue straight on to Criquebeuf-en-Caux.

Continue north-eastwards towards Grainval. As you leave the village, you will find that the GR is not marked for the first 700 metres. However, the markings reappear above Grainval. The route descends and then rises again, going past a restaurant. At the top carry straight on, turning left when you reach a campsite. Cross the campsite and continue to Fécamp.

Find your way to the north quay and leave Fécamp by the Matelots footpath, which is to the west of the quay. The GR follows road D79 until it reaches a crossroads (see IGN map 150 000 ref 106). From there turn left and head towards Le Val-Ausson.

Alternative route from Fécamp to La Val-de-la-Mer. When the Matelots path reaches a signal tower branch off left along the cliffs to Le Val-de-la-Mer. The stretch of coast between Le Val-de-la-Mer and Le Val-Ausson is dangerous and should not be attempted. Instead, at Le Val-de-la-Mer, turn right and go up the valley to the D79. Turn left along this road until you reach a crossroads (see map IGN ref 106).

Shortly after the alternative route rejoins the D79, you reach a crossroads (see map IGN ref

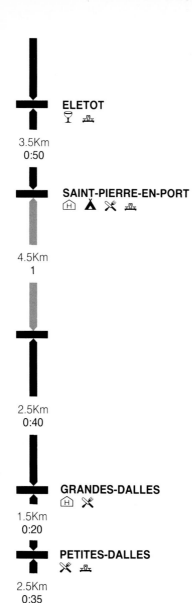

ELETOT

3.5Km
0:50

SAINT-PIERRE-EN-PORT

4.5Km
1

2.5Km
0:40

GRANDES-DALLES

1.5Km
0:20

PETITES-DALLES

2.5Km
0:35

SASSETOT-LE-MAUCONDUIT

2.5Km
0:35
Junction with the alternative route from Saint-Pierre-en-Port.

106). Turn left to Le Val-Ausson. Go through Le Val-Ausson. You will find that the GR way-markings start again 200 metres from the sea. Continue along the GR to the village of Élétot.

The GR goes through Élétot and continues in a north-east direction along a dirt track. When the track ends, you will see the belfry of Saint-Pierre-en-Port. Go towards it. When you reach the edge of the wood, take the steep-sided narrow way down to Saint-Pierre-en-Port.

Alternative route from St-Pierre-en-Port to Sassetot-le-Mauconduit. From the top of the steps leading up from the beach, swing right towards the church. Now cross towards the water-tower (see map IGN ref 93) and take the path down to the bottom of the Hetre valley. At the bottom, turn right, up the valley, until your path intersects with a small road. Turn left along the road, which will take you to Sassetot-le-Mauconduit.

From the beach at Saint-Pierre-en-Port, continue along the GR21 by taking the steps leading up from the beach. At the top, turn left towards the cliff-top. Pass the houses and take the dirt track heading north-east. When you reach the point where a path comes up from the D79, walk 25 metres to the left and then turn right. When the GR reaches the edge of the valley, turn left and then right, before continuing down to the hamlet of Les Grandes-Dalles.

The GR leaves the hamlet opposite the fountain and heads north, skirting a field and then continuing along the cliffs to Petites-Dalles.

When you come to the first houses, keep to the right and continue through the wood as far as the hamlet of Houlgate. From there, take the D5, right, past the château, then turn left in front of the church.

Continue until you reach a fork where the D5 meets the D479. Take the footpath to the left past the outbuildings of the château until it joins a small road. Turn right along the road to Vinnemerville.

131

Vinnemerville

2.5Km
0:35

Butot-Vénesville
Detour, *30 mins*
TOURNETOT
⌂
On the edge of Vénesville
take the D71 road (north-
west) towards Saint-Martin-
aux-Buneaux.

2Km
0:35

Road D68
Detour, *15 mins*
AUBERVILLE-LA-
MANUEL
✕ ♟
At the junction with the D68,
you can make a detour to the
village of
Auberville-la-Manuel (see
left). 16th–17th century
château.

4Km
1

VEULETTES-SUR-MER
⌂ ▲ ✕ ⚓ 🚃
❼

5Km
1:15

Conteville

9Km
2:15

Take the small road to the left of the church and continue to the *mairie* at Butot-Vénesville.

The GR turns left beyond the *mairie*. Go through the hamlet of Sainte-Ville and join the Grand Val path which heads north towards the sea. After a while you come to the D68.

The GR21 does not enter the village; it continues down the Grand Val path to the edge of Veulettes-sur-Mer. Turn right here and go up through the woods. After crossing the D271 the GR follows the crest of La Falaisette, providing views of the beach and the Durdent valley, and then descends to the beach at Veulettes-sur-Mer.

From Veulettes the GR21 follows the same south-easterly route along the left bank of the Durdent as the GR211. At the edge of Paluel they split up: the GR211 leads south-east towards Cany-Barville; while the GR21 turns left towards the centre of Paluel. Take the path on the left of the church up past the chapel, then at the Janville water-tower turn left along a dirt track until you reach the road to Conteville.

Alternative route from Veulettes to Conteville (unmarked). Take the D10 heading north-east and cross the River Durdent. At the hamlet of Pont-Rouge, turn left along a footpath which takes you up to the plateau. Now bear right until you rejoin the GR21 by the château at Conteville.

Follow the GR21 past the château, and turn right. Continue, until you reach the road to Bertheauville. Turn left, and then take the D79 to the right. Pass the Paluel electricity sub-station, then turn left (north-west) on to a dirt track. At the first junction take the road right (north-east) past Le Tot to Saint-Léger. From there take the cliff-top path to Saint-Valéry-en-Caux.

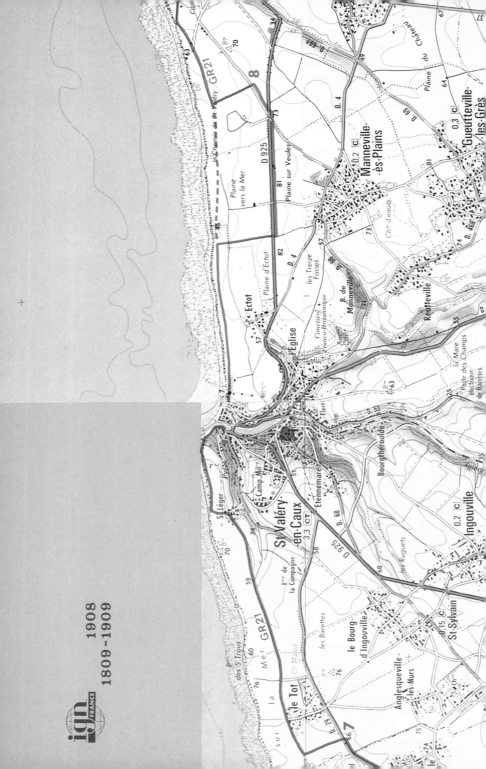

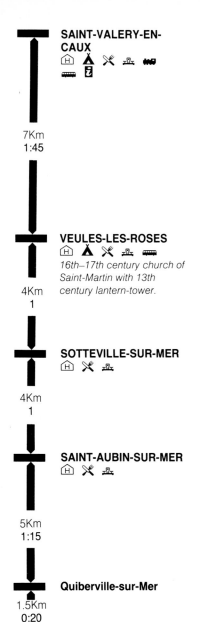

SAINT-VALERY-EN-CAUX

7Km
1:45

Take the coastal path east out of Saint-Valéry-en-Caux for 2 kilometres along the cliff-top. At the moment, it is impossible to follow the coast path all the way from Saint-Valéry to Quiberville, therefore you should follow the diversions signposted in yellow. Turn right along the edge of a field, following the yellow markings, first to a dirt track, and then to the D925; turn left and walk along the road for 1.6 kilometres. Take a surfaced track north-east. After 300 metres, turn left again on to a footpath which leads you back to the cliff-top. Turn right along the path, which runs parallel to the shore, and continue on to Veules-les-Roses.

VEULES-LES-ROSES

16th–17th century church of Saint-Martin with 13th century lantern-tower.

4Km
1

Go south out of Veules-les-Roses through narrow streets along the river. At the main road junction take the D925 towards Rouen, and after 50 metres turn left on to a small path which runs between houses. At the top turn right and then, after 500 metres, turn left on to a paved path which crosses the D68 before coming to Sotteville-sur-Mer.

SOTTEVILLE-SUR-MER

4Km
1

Leave Sotteville by heading towards the sea. Take the paved path, right, along the coast for 1.5 kilometres. Turn right on to the path which leads back to the D68. Before you reach Le Mesnil-Gaillard, bear left along the road which takes you through Épineville and on to Saint-Aubin-sur-Mer.

SAINT-AUBIN-SUR-MER

5Km
1:15

The GR21 rejoins the coastline at Saint-Aubin-sur-Mer. Continue north-east along the coast and turn right on to the only track which runs along the valley. Marked in white and yellow, the track passes through the small village of Ramouville to Flainville, where there is a chapel on the farm. Here, take the first road on the left, which crosses the D75 to reach Quiberville-sur-Mer.

Quiberville-sur-Mer

1.5Km
0:20

Follow the GR through the village to the beach, then continue north-east along the D75 until you come to the GR212.

Junction with GR212

1Km
0:15

The GR212 heads right (south-east) towards Pavilly, while the GR21 leaves the D75 and continues along a footpath which leads uphill to Sainte-Marguerite.

SAINTE-MARGUERITE

⌂ ✕ ⍭ ⚓

This picturesque village has attracted many visiting artists. 12th–16th century church. Local footpath, way-marked in yellow, to Le Hamelet, via Manor of Ango.

8Km
2

Le Hamelet

Detour, *1.5Km, 20 mins.*

Saint-Aubin

West of the château at Le Hamelet a route waymarked in yellow leads to the Manoir d'Ango and back to Sainte-Marguerite.

2Km
0:30

Chapel with stained-glass windows by Braque, on D75; 16th century manor, Le Manoir d'Ango.

POURVILLE-SUR-MER

7.5Km   ⌂ ✕
2

DIEPPE

⌂ ⌂ ⛺ ✕ ⍭

⚓ ⛴

Dieppe is the nearest coastal resort to Paris and has fishing, commercial, and passenger docks.
15th century château-museum, with unique collection of carved ivory figures; panoramic view from chapel of Notre-Dame-de-Bon-Secours; 14th–16th century church of Saint-Jacques; church of Saint-Rémy.

The GR21 goes through Sainte-Marguerite. At the church, take the road (east) through the wood. When you reach a water-tower, turn left towards the Ailly lighthouse. Turn right there, along a road which leads past some houses and down through the wooded valley. At the bottom of the valley, take the dirt track opposite which leads to the D27. Follow the D27 to the left towards a naval cemetery and a church. Before you reach the cemetery, take the footpath on the right, which runs next to the Park of Les Moutiers. Bear south and, continuing through the undergrowth, take the footpath on the left. This brings you to the small village of Rue-de-l'Aumône, where you turn left on to a path which leads eastwards down to a deeply-sunken track. Cross the track and continue along the footpath through the woodland to Le Hamelet.

From Le Hamelet the GR21 passes to the north of the château and takes the road (north-east) leading to the beach at Pourville-sur-Mer.

From Pourville-sur-Mer take the D75 (north-east) to the château at Dieppe.

Alternative route from Pourville-sur-Mer to Dieppe. Walk along the D153 south-east from Pourville for 300 metres. Bear right on to a track (south) which leads upwards to Bernouville. Follow the path, to the left, passing in front of a water-tower. When you reach the D153, turn right on to the road. Go through Petit-Appeville, where there is a railway halt, crossing the railway line by the bridge. Go straight along the footpath up to the Canadian cemetery, then continue to the crossroads (see map IGN ref 88) and turn left (north). Your route will take you through the Janval district (see left).

INDEX

The many different kinds of accommodation in France are explained in the introduction. Here we include a selection of hotels and other addresses, which is by no means exhaustive — the hotels listed are usually in the one-star or two-star categories. We have given full postal addresses so bookings can be made.

There has been an explosive growth in bed and breakfast facilities (chambres d'hôte) in the past few years, and staying in these private homes can be especially interesting and rewarding. Local shops and the town hall (mairie) can usually direct you to one.

Details of bus/train connections have been provided wherever it was possible. We suggest you refer also to the map inside the front cover.